D1563369

# Child Maltreatment Solutions Network

**Series editor**

Jennie G. Noll
Pennsylvania State University, University Park, PA, USA

More information about this series at http://www.springer.com/series/15457

Carlomagno C. Panlilio
Editor

# Trauma-Informed Schools

Integrating Child Maltreatment Prevention,
Detection, and Intervention

 Springer

*Editor*
Carlomagno C. Panlilio
Pennsylvania State University
University Park, PA, USA

ISSN 2509-7156          ISSN 2509-7164   (electronic)
Child Maltreatment Solutions Network
ISBN 978-3-030-12810-4          ISBN 978-3-030-12811-1   (eBook)
https://doi.org/10.1007/978-3-030-12811-1

Library of Congress Control Number: 2019936171

This Springer imprint is published by the registered company Springer Nature Switzerland AG
The registered company address is: Gewerbestrasse 11, 6330 Cham, Switzerland

# Acknowledgments

As part of its outreach mission, the Child Maltreatment Solutions Network holds annual conferences on important topics related to child maltreatment prevention and the promotion of child well-being. In organizing the Network's first conference on how to bring about trauma-informed systems into schools, I wanted to invite presenters and contributors who could impart valuable knowledge and exciting new research in the field. I am therefore grateful to this group of presenters and contributors for sharing their expertise and leading a dialogue on emergent issues around trauma-informed schools during the conference. I would also like to thank each one of the authors for their contributions and commitment to this book. I am deeply grateful for your willingness, time, and expertise to extend our conference dialogue about trauma-informed schools to a broader audience.

I am grateful to the Child Maltreatment Solutions Network for the opportunity to organize the conference and serve as an editor for this volume. I would like to thank Jennie Noll for her leadership of the Network, especially for her dedication to the cause of improving the lives of children. I would also like to thank Sandee Kyler, assistant director of the Network, for her dedication and persistence in ensuring that the conference and this book came to fruition. I would like to thank Cheri McConnell, education coordinator for the Network, for ensuring that the conference was well-organized. Many thanks to my faculty colleagues at the Network for your support and dedication during the conference and beyond.

I am also grateful to the Social Science Research Institute at the Pennsylvania State University and especially to Susan McHale, for her visionary leadership in bringing together a cadre of interdisciplinary scientists to understand and find solutions to the problems associated with child maltreatment. I would also like to extend my gratitude to the College of Education and especially to our dean, David Monk, for his ongoing support and leadership for interdisciplinary work that brings education at the forefront of child well-being.

Finally, I would like to say thank you to the sponsors of the conference: the Edna Bennett Pierce Prevention Research Center; the Child Study Center; the Clearinghouse for Military Family Readiness; the Clinical and Translational Science Institute; the College of Nursing; the Department of Biobehavioral Health; the

Department of Educational Psychology, Counseling, and Special Education; the Department of Human Development and Family Studies; and the Penn State Public Health Sciences. Their ongoing support and involvement ensures that we continue to engage in interdisciplinary work to ensure the promotion of children's well-being.

# Introduction to Trauma-Informed Schools

The developmental changes across physical, cognitive, and socioemotional domains rely heavily on the quality of children's relationships with the adults in their lives. In the face of traumatic events, whether they are witnessed or pose a direct threat, children's resilience and capacity to cope are inundated, which have deleterious effects across many domains of functioning inside and outside of the classroom. These difficulties can negatively affect educational well-being and often persist over the long term, creating unnecessary barriers to learning and later independence. This is a particularly salient issue given the estimate that one out of every four students in US schools has been exposed to acute or chronic traumatic events according to the National Child Traumatic Stress Network (NCTSN, 2018). It is during these acute or chronic traumatic moments that children depend on knowledgeable and caring adults to provide a sense of safety that buffers the negative effects of traumatic experiences. Given the importance of these adult-child relationships, school personnel and particularly teachers are important and necessary partners in identifying and responding to the unique challenges of childhood trauma. By providing students with a sense of safety and support and promoting a readiness to learn in the context of trauma, schools become an important place wherein students can thrive and achieve.

Given the challenges related to childhood trauma and its impact on development and learning, the need to incorporate trauma-informed approaches in schools is imperative. According to the NCTSN (2018), a trauma-informed system is broadly defined as any child- and family-serving system that recognizes and responds to the impact of traumatic stress on children, as well as the caregivers, staff, and other providers who are part of that system. Trauma-informed schools in particular include the recognition of, and the need to respond to, the impact of traumatic experiences on students' academic-related competencies, including achievement measures, socioemotional skills, and mental health, among others. Trauma-informed school systems also recognize that traumatic stress may affect other school-related stakeholders such as families or caregivers, teachers, administrators, and other school staff. The NCTSN provides a specific system framework that schools from pre-K-12 can follow in order to implement system-wide changes that acknowledge the role of trauma in educational achievement. The trauma-informed school system framework includes core areas wherein schools can focus their efforts for organizational changes and improvement.

The framework is drawn from a multi-tiered system of support (MTSS) approach most often used in the early identification of, and provision of support for, students with learning and emotional or behavioral needs. Core elements of a trauma-informed school can be applied across all support system levels to create a trauma-informed school environment. Tier 1 includes universal prevention efforts that create and sustain a trauma-informed school community that provides safe environments for students, caregivers, educators, and other important stakeholders. Tier 2 includes efforts for early identification of and intervention services for students and staff at risk in order to prevent further negative cascading effects on multiple domains of functioning. Finally, Tier 3 includes intensive support services, such as trauma-specific interventions that would help alleviate any potential negative effects of trauma exposure. According to the 2017 NCTSN System Framework (National Child Traumatic Stress Network, Schools Committee, 2017), there are ten core elements of trauma-informed school systems that include:

1. Identification and assessment of traumatic stress
2. Prevention and intervention related to traumatic stress
3. Trauma education and awareness
4. Partnership with students and families
5. Creation of a trauma-informed learning environment
6. Cultural responsiveness
7. Emergency management/crisis response
8. Staff self-care and secondary traumatic stress
9. School discipline policies and practices
10. Cross-system collaboration and community partnerships

These core elements are integral in the creation of trauma-informed schools that can provide the necessary support for students affected by acute or chronic traumatic events succeed in their educational pursuits. Given the importance of instituting a trauma-informed system of care within the school context, an important next step is to bring together a panel of important stakeholders to discuss how integration should proceed. The conference "Trauma-Informed Schools: How Child Maltreatment Prevention, Detection, and Intervention Can Be Integrated into the School Setting" became the venue to pursue this specific goal. The conference, which was held on October 10–11, 2016, at the Pennsylvania State University's Nittany Lion Inn, brought together key members of the research, education, social welfare, and other child-serving communities to engage in transdisciplinary dialogue. Ideally, this would help to transform knowledge into workable, practical solutions for students, teachers, and community stakeholders. More specifically, our panel of scientists, educators, administrators, and advocates, along with some committed and selfless attendees on the front lines of serving maltreated children, came together to explore how schools can more effectively move toward a coordinated, multifaceted trauma-informed approach to education that is guided by the 2017

NCTSN System Framework for Trauma-Informed Schools. This volume reflects the conversations that took place during those few days dedicated to improving the educational well-being of traumatized students.

The purpose of this volume, therefore, is to serve as a resource for understanding which elements of trauma-informed schools should be taken into consideration by education leaders, practitioners, and researchers. Mary Pulido's chapter introduces the *Safe Touches* program, a school-based sexual abuse prevention workshop for culturally and socioeconomically diverse students across kindergarten and third grade. Claire Crooks and David Wolfe's section discusses the Fourth R program that aims to teach healthy relationships and decrease risky behaviors in students between 7th and 12th grades. The Fourth R curriculum was developed to be culturally and socioeconomically relevant and provides educators with the tools to address school- and home-based concerns. Taken together, these chapters provide the reader with exemplary programs that fit within a Tier 1, universal prevention approach to ensure safety for students. At the same time, these programs meet several of the NCTSN core elements for trauma-informed schools: prevention and intervention, education and awareness, partnerships with students and families, and cultural responsiveness.

Brenda Jones Harden, Laura Jimenez Parra, and Aimee Drouin Duncan examine the sequelae of experiencing early adversity across multiple domains of functioning in children and discuss the implications of early trauma exposure for school-based interventions, particularly within a trauma-informed framework. The authors provide an in-depth discussion on how to translate knowledge about the developmental sequelae of trauma across Tiers 1–3 and how schools can respond accordingly. Specifically, the authors present recommendations that address several core elements for trauma-informed schools: identification and assessment, prevention and intervention, trauma education and awareness, partnerships with students and families, and the creation of a trauma-informed learning environment. Carlomagno Panlilio, Amanda Ferrara, and Leigha MacNeill explore the relationship between early adversity, self-regulation, and learning from the perspectives of developmental science and educational psychology. They specifically argue for more proximal and dynamic views of learning as a framework to understand mechanisms that lead to educational challenges that maltreated children experience. This discussion provides important next steps that can inform the fifth core element of trauma-informed schools: the creation of a trauma-informed learning environment. Additionally, the content in these two chapters can be used in professional development workshops to better understand the impact of trauma on development and learning, addressing the core element of trauma education and awareness.

Susan Stone discusses the need to frame our understanding of maltreatment as a "wicked problem" fraught with complex and unclear solutions that require the involvement of stakeholders. Framing the social problem of maltreatment as "wicked" requires acknowledging the role that schools and other child-serving systems of care may play in responding. Therefore, there is a need for coordination and collaboration across stakeholders and institutions to address the educational needs of maltreated children within educational settings. Stone's discussion presents a perspective from which to consider the multiple contexts relevant to children who experience early maltreatment, addressing two core elements of trauma-informed systems: prevention and intervention across stakeholders and cross-system collaboration and community partnerships.

Christy Tirrell-Corbin provides an in-depth look at macro- and micro-level educational responses to childhood trauma. She discusses current mandated reporting practices in education as well as resulting secondary stress in teachers. Christy also provides recommendations for the creation of trauma-sensitive pedagogies and examples of how this might be approached at the preservice teacher preparation and in-service professional development levels. The discussions around school micro- and macro-level responses address several core elements of trauma-informed schools that include trauma education and awareness, partnerships with students and families, the creation of a trauma-informed learning environment, and staff self-care and secondary stress.

Taken together, the topics in this book are important to consider when implementing trauma-informed practices in schools. However, what will be presented is not an exhaustive list of solutions that covers the full range of NCTSN's core elements, but a starting point from which the conference's dialogue may be continued. Our goal for this volume, therefore, is to encourage our readers to consider the elements of trauma-informed schools as presented across the chapters and to use this volume as an intellectual springboard. By acknowledging the role that early adversity plays in children's development and learning and incorporating support from dedicated educators in the field, we can begin to help traumatized children move toward educational well-being and academic success.

# References

National Child Traumatic Stress Network. (2018). Retrieved November 30, 2018, from https://www.nctsn.org/what-is-child-trauma/about-child-trauma

National Child Traumatic Stress Network, Schools Committee. (2017). Creating, supporting, and sustaining trauma-informed schools: A system framework. Los Angeles, CA, and Durham, NC: National Center for Child Traumatic Stress. Retrieved from https://www.nctsn.org/sites/default/files/resources//creating_supporting_sustaining_trauma_informed_schools_a_systems_framework.pdf

The Pennsylvania State University                                    Carlomagno C. Panlilio
State College, PA, USA

# Contents

# About the Editor

**Carlomagno C. Panlilio, Ph.D.** is an assistant professor in the Department of Educational Psychology, Counseling, and Special Education and a faculty member with the Child Maltreatment Solutions Network at the Pennsylvania State University. The overarching goal of Dr. Panlilio's program of research is to understand the dynamic interplay between maltreatment, context, and development and how these processes influence individual differences in learning. His research is guided by an interdisciplinary approach that draws from developmental science, educational psychology, statistics, and social welfare to examine the multisystemic influences on early adversity and children's learning. More specifically, he is interested in further explicating self-regulation and self-regulated learning as key developmental and learning processes that explain variability in the academic outcomes of children with a history of maltreatment. Prior to his faculty appointment, Dr. Panlilio practiced as a licensed clinical marriage and family therapist. He has worked in private practice, community agencies, treatment foster care, and a residential treatment facility for adolescents. He has been in clinical practice since 2005 and often worked with at-risk children and families. He previously served as the vice chair for the Maryland Board of Professional Counselors and Therapists and also served as the chair for the Ethics Committee. Dr. Panlilio earned his B.A. in Psychology from the California State University at Long Beach and an M.S. in Family Studies with a concentration in Couple and Family Therapy from the University of Maryland, College Park. Dr. Panlilio earned his Ph.D. in Developmental Science and a certificate in Education, Measurement, and Statistics from the University of Maryland, College Park.

# About the Authors

**Claire V. Crooks, Ph.D.** is an associate professor at the Faculty of Education at Western University and the director of the Centre for School Mental Health. She is one of the lead developers and researchers of the *Fourth R*, the relationship-based program aimed at preventing violence and related risk behaviors among adolescents. She is particularly interested in adaptation and implementation issues related to evidence-based practices. Her work in this area includes development and evaluation of strategies that meet the unique needs of Indigenous youth and other priority groups. Dr. Crooks provides continuing education to judges, lawyers, and other court professionals as a faculty member for the US National Council of Juvenile and Family Court Judges. She is coauthor of more than 80 articles, chapters, and books on topics including school-based programming with Indigenous youth, children's exposure to domestic violence, child custody and access, adolescent dating violence and risk behavior, and trauma. Dr. Crooks completed her undergraduate education at Princeton University and then went to Queen's University for her M.A. and Ph.D. She is a clinical psychologist and is registered in the areas of clinical, school, and forensic psychology.

**Aimee Drouin Duncan, Ph.D.** is an applied developmental psychologist studying the effects of environmental risk on development. She has worked with children, families, and caseworkers involved in the child welfare system. She has also been involved in early intervention administration and research. She is interested in high-risk children and families served by child welfare and other public service agencies to support evidence-based practice and promote positive child outcomes. Recently she completed a policy fellowship with the Society for Research in Child Development (SRCD) to promote the use of evidence-based decision-making in government administration to serve children and families, including the most vulnerable to trauma and receiving intervention services. She seeks to continue strengthening the links between evidence-based policy, practice, and philanthropy. Dr. Drouin Duncan received her Ph.D. in Developmental Science from the University of Maryland, College Park.

Amanda Ferrara   is currently a doctoral candidate in the Educational Psychology program at the Pennsylvania State University. She earned a Bachelor of Science in Psychology and a Bachelor of Arts in Philosophy from the University of Pittsburgh. Amanda has worked as a public school teacher as well as a research assistant benefitting preservice teachers and military families.

**Brenda Jones Harden, Ph.D.** is a professor in the Department of Human Development and Quantitative Methodology, University of Maryland, College Park. She has worked for over 35 years in the early childhood policy, practice, and research arenas. Her research examines the developmental and mental health needs of young children at environmental risk, particularly those who have been maltreated or exposed to other forms of trauma. A particular focus is preventing maladaptive outcomes in these populations through early childhood and parenting programs, such as early care and education, home visiting services, and infant mental health interventions. Dr. Jones Harden is the author of numerous publications regarding vulnerable children and families, particularly risk and protective factors that are linked with their developmental and mental health outcomes. She also has conducted numerous implementation and impact evaluations of early childhood and prevention programs. Dr. Jones Harden is the sole author of the book *Infants in the Child Welfare System: A Developmental Perspective on Policy and Practice*, a coauthor of *Beyond Common Sense: Child Welfare, Child Well-Being, and the Evidence for Policy Reform*, and a coeditor of *Child Welfare and Child Well-Being: New Perspectives from the National Survey of Child and Adolescent Well-Being*. As a scientist-practitioner, Dr. Jones Harden uses research to inform the development of interventions to improve the outcomes of vulnerable children and their families. She regularly provides training and consultation to early childhood, parenting, and other intervention programs to improve the quality of services provided to young children and families experiencing trauma and other forms of environmental risk. During much of her career, she was a practitioner working with maltreated children and families. She has directed two programs to prevent child abuse and neglect and has also worked as a foster care and adoption social worker. Dr. Jones Harden received her Doctoral Degree in Developmental and Clinical Psychology from Yale University and a Master's Degree in Social Work from New York University.

**Leigha MacNeill, M.S.** is a doctoral candidate in the Developmental Psychology program at the Pennsylvania State University. She received her B.A. in Psychology and English from the University of Rochester in 2012. Her research aims to integrate family systems models and biological perspectives to investigate children's self-regulation across multiple levels of analysis. Specifically, she is interested in studying how factors extrinsic (e.g., family, socioeconomic status or SES) and intrinsic (e.g., child temperament, biology) to the child contribute to their development of self-regulation over time, as well as how these regulatory trajectories can place children at risk for internalizing problems. By taking a family systems perspective, she examines how different yet interconnected subsystems (e.g., marital, coparenting, parent-child, sibling) shape changes in children's socioemotional development over time. Her dissertation examines the interplay of parenting and child temperament in the development of attention processes in infancy and early childhood, leveraging stationary eye-tracking, mobile eye-tracking, and electroencephalography measures of attention. Her work has been published in *Child Development*.

**Laura Jimenez Parra** is currently a third-year doctoral student in the Department of Human Development and Quantitative Methodology at the University of Maryland, College Park. Her research interests focus on the effects of intervention and prevention programs on young children's socioemotional development, specifically centering on the impact these have on Latino low-income children's academic success. Through collecting developmental, behavioral, physiological, and self-report data from high-risk families in their homes, she has direct knowledge of the sequelae of trauma exposure and the protective factors of these intervention and prevention programs.

**Mary L. Pulido, Ph.D.** is executive director of The New York Society for the Prevention of Cruelty to Children, the first child protective agency in the world. The NYSPCC provides mental health, legal, and educational services for children, families, and professionals involved in the child protection arena. She has served as a principal investigator for a research study on child sexual abuse prevention for the National Institutes of Health (NIH). She has held senior management positions at the Child Advocacy Center of Montefiore Medical Center; The Children's Village, a long-term residential treatment facility for abused children; and Covenant House/Under 21, a crisis shelter for homeless children. She is also a Medical Reserve Corps "first responder" to disaster trauma through the NYC Department of Health and Mental Hygiene and served as a member of the New York City Child Fatality Review Advisory Team from 2006 to 2015. She currently serves as president of the New York State Professional Society on the Abuse of Children (APSAC-NY). Dr. Pulido has a Ph.D. in Social Welfare from the City University of New York, a Master's Degree in Social Work from Hunter College, and a Master's Degree in Teaching from Sacred Heart University. Dr. Pulido holds the rank of adjunct assistant professor at the Silberman School of Social Work at Hunter College. She has published in the areas of crisis debriefing, prevention of child sexual abuse, trauma recovery, supervised visitation, and managing and preventing secondary traumatic stress. She is a blogger for Huffington Post on child protection issues.

**Susan Stone, Ph.D.** is an associate professor and the Catherine Mary and Eileen Clare Hutto Chair for Social Services in Public Education at the University of California at Berkeley. She received her B.A. in Behavioral Science and her A.M. and Ph.D. degrees from the School of Social Service Administration at the University of Chicago. Her substantive area of interest lies in the intersection of social welfare and education. Specifically, she is interested in (1) the educational experiences of underserved student subgroups (e.g., youth involved in foster care and other human service systems), (2) how school organizational and institutional features shape student experiences in schools, (3) the organization and arrangement of school-based social service delivery systems, and (4) the attributes of school social work practice and its relationship to student and school academic performance. Her research typically draws upon school administrative data sources, with attention to methods to extract causally informative information from observational data sources. She has most recently been engaged in collaborations with the San Francisco Unified School District to leverage administrative data to better understand district- and school-level social and related service delivery dynamics. A listing of her publications can be found here: http://tinyurl.com/Stone-Publications

**Christy Tirrell-Corbin, Ph.D.** is the executive director of the University of Maryland (UMD), Center for Early Childhood Education and Intervention (CECEI), and the director of the UMD Early Childhood/Early Childhood Special Education (EC/ECSE) Program. Her research interests focus on young children at environmental risk due to poverty, teachers in high-poverty communities, and family engagement. She has done extensive work with in-service teachers in Title I communities around strategies to increase family engagement in culturally and contextually responsive ways. Earlier in her career, Dr. Tirrell-Corbin worked in foster care and adoption in New York City, where she served as a casework manager and facilitated workshops for both biological and adoptive parents. Dr. Tirrell-Corbin was the project director/principal investigator for CECEI's evaluation of Maryland's Race to the Top Early Learning Challenge Grant and is currently the principal investigator on projects focused on family engagement, professional development, and inquiry-based curricula for children birth to 5. She is the co-principal investigator on an evaluation of the District of Columbia, Quality Improvement Network, funded through an Early Head Start Grant. Dr. Tirrell-Corbin has served as a consultant for a number of organizations that include PBS Kids and National Geographic.

**David A. Wolfe, Ph.D.** is a psychologist and author specializing in issues affecting children and youth, with a special focus on child abuse, dating violence, and mental health and well-being. He was a professor of Psychology at Western University from 1980 to 2002, where he was the co-founder and academic director of the Centre for Research and Education on Violence Against Women and Children in their Faculty of Education. In 2002, he was awarded the inaugural RBC Chair in Children's Mental Health at the Centre for Addiction and Mental Health (CAMH) and the University of Toronto. With support from numerous grants and donors, he started the Centre for Prevention Science located in London, Ontario, in 2004, where he conducts research on school-based strategies to prevent adolescent risk behaviors. His recent books include *Adolescent Risk Behaviors: Why Teens Experiment and Strategies to Keep Them Safe* (with P. Jaffe and C. Crooks; Yale University Press, 2006) and *Growing Up with Domestic Violence: Assessment, Intervention & Prevention Strategies for Children & Adolescents* (with P. Jaffe and M. Campbell; Hogrefe & Huber, 2011). He is also the coauthor (with Eric Mash) of *Abnormal Child Psychology* (Cengage, 2015), a popular university textbook in its sixth edition. He served as editor-in-chief of *Child Abuse & Neglect: The International Journal* from 2007 to 2013. Dr. Wolfe has been pioneering new approaches to preventing many societal youth problems such as bullying, relationship violence, and substance abuse through universal education programs. Along with his Western colleagues Peter Jaffe and Claire Crooks, he developed and evaluated the *Fourth R*, a school-based program to promote healthy relationships and well-being among children and youth. The *Fourth R* is currently taught in over 5000 schools in Canada and the USA and has been identified as a promising violence prevention strategy by numerous reviews of evidence-based programs for youth. His work has been recognized by UNESCO and several professional associations for his contributions to the elimination of violence against women and children.

# Chapter 1
# *Safe Touches*: Creating a School Community to Prevent Child Sexual Abuse

Mary L. Pulido

## 1.1 Overview of The New York Society for the Prevention of Cruelty to Children

Founded in 1875, The New York Society for the Prevention of Cruelty to Children (NYSPCC) was the first child protection agency in the world. The NYSPCC developed the basic tenets of child protection laws in the United States and has worked tirelessly for the past 142 years to improve the safety of children. Guided by its mission—to respond to the complex needs of abused and neglected children, and those involved in their care, by providing best-practice counseling, legal, and educational services—The NYSPCC has served over two million children.

Today, The NYSPCC remains steadfast in assisting high-risk children and families and currently emphasizes programs aimed at the prevention of child maltreatment and the lessening of its harmful effects. Programs include a mixture of preventive and treatment services.

I. *Intervention/Treatment*

- Counseling for children—The Trauma Recovery Program helps children to recover from experiences of physical abuse, sexual abuse, family violence, traumatic grief, or parental neglect through mental health services for them and their caregivers.
- Strengthen and rebuild families—The Therapeutic Supervised Visitation Program serves families who are referred to The NYSPCC when a family court judge determines that a parent cannot be left unsupervised with their children due to safety concerns. This program promotes healthy parenting

M. L. Pulido (✉)
The New York Society for the Prevention of Cruelty to Children, New York, NY, USA
e-mail: MPulido@nyspcc.org

© Springer Nature Switzerland AG 2019
C. C. Panlilio (ed.), *Trauma-Informed Schools*, Child Maltreatment Solutions Network, https://doi.org/10.1007/978-3-030-12811-1_1

skills through supervised visits between parents and children, one-on-one coaching, and parent education workshops.

- Counseling for child welfare professionals—Crisis Debriefing counseling supports child protective staff at the NYC Administration for Children's Services (ACS) and other child welfare agencies following incidents of child fatality, violence in the field, and during times of bereavement.

II. *Prevention/Education*

- Education for children—The NYSPCC brings its *Safe Touches* child sexual abuse prevention workshops to children in grades kindergarten through 12 in NYC schools.
- Training for organizations and professionals—The NYSPCC Training Institute educates child welfare professionals, teachers, the corporate sector, community organizations, and parent groups. Topics include child abuse prevention, identifying and reporting child abuse and neglect, best-practice models of service provision, and managing secondary traumatic stress.
- Advocacy and raising public awareness—The NYSPCC takes an active role, both as an individual agency and in coalition with others, to educate the general public and support legislation that will improve the protection of children from abuse and neglect.
- Research and evaluation—The NYSPCC conducts rigorous research and evaluation to inform best practices both within the agency and in the broader child welfare field.

Programs are offered at multiple sites, including The NYSPCC's main office in Lower Manhattan, NYC public schools, foster care, and other social service agencies. Bilingual services (English and Spanish) are provided to families 7 days and 3 evenings per week to accommodate working parents and meet the ever-increasing demand for its programs. The NYSPCC does not charge families for direct program services, and no family in need is ever turned away. In 2016, The NYSPCC served over 10,000 children, parents, caregivers, and professionals.

### 1.1.1 The Need for Child Sexual Abuse Prevention Programs

Child sexual abuse is a chronic, underreported tragedy in the United States. Studies cited by Prevent Child Abuse America estimate that at least 20% of American women and 5–16% of American men experienced some form of sexual abuse as children (Finkelhor, 1994). Victims of child sexual abuse experience a myriad of physical and mental health problems that often persist through adulthood. More than two decades of research has linked child sexual abuse to increased rates of pregnancy, promiscuity, low self-esteem, obesity, anxiety, depression, anger, aggression, post-traumatic stress, dissociation, hallucinations, sexual difficulties, self-injurious behaviors, substance abuse, coronary artery disease, and permanent changes in neurobiological functioning (Finkelhor, 1990; Neumann, Houskamp, Pollock, & Briere, 1996; Noll, Zeller, Trickett, & Putnam, 2007; Putnam, 2003).

The NYSPCC stresses to the public that CSA can occur in all populations, in all socioeconomic and educational levels, and across all racial and cultural groups. It is often perpetrated by someone the child knows and is comfortable with, such as a family member or another trusted adult. The inability of children to recognize abuse; the fear and anxiety of reporting abuse when children do recognize it; and the prevalence of internet solicitation of children reflect an ever-growing need to teach children how to identify and report sexual abuse. Children need to be educated about their bodies and feelings and should be able to distinguish between touches that are safe and those that are not safe in order to reduce the incidence and effects of this devastating type of abuse.

Based on my experience at The NYSPCC, most parents do not have conversations with their children as regularly as they should about protection and child safety. Children—or, at least, those who have been counseled in our Trauma Recovery Program—often did not disclose CSA for at least a year after the incident occurred; for some, the time until disclosure was longer. This means that in addition to the trauma endured by the child, the perpetrator of the abuse may not have been held accountable and may still be abusing other children. Additionally, I also have the privilege of speaking to many adult survivors who have joined with our efforts to help promote *Safe Touches*. Many survivors have expressed that they wished there was a program like *Safe Touches* when they were children so that they would have known what to do when they were approached and how to protect themselves.

## 1.1.2 Responding to NYC Schools

High-profile stories of CSA, including allegations made against teachers and other staff in NYC schools, and religious communities protecting authority figures who have allegedly abused children have underscored the need for education of children, teachers, staff, and parents.

The NYSPCC has a history of building relationships with the New York City public school system. When there is a crisis regarding CSA, The NYSPCC meets with and provide appropriate training to the guidance counselors, the teachers, the principal, and the parents. The NYSPCC is very responsive to their requests and tailored our program to their needs. In New York City, the Citywide Coordinator for Child Abuse and Neglect Prevention in the NYC Department of Education is responsible for overseeing all child abuse prevention for the public school system. We formed an alliance with the staff so that whenever there is an incident for which they needed our help, they were able to call us. This office reported to the chancellor's office. This prior working relationship also assisted us when we were ready to launch the National Institutes of Health (NIH) research project, as they knew our work and were familiar with our clinicians; we had provided workshops to children, teachers, and parent associations after incidents of child sexual abuse.

In response to the prevalence of this horrific, underreported crime, The NYSPCC has developed a range of child protection, education, and administrative review services for NYC public, private, and charter schools, including:

- Age-appropriate child sexual abuse prevention training for students in grades K–12.
- Child abuse identification and reporting procedures training for faculty and staff.
- Reviews of schools' current policies and procedures regarding child protective issues and recommendations for amendments or additions that would strengthen these services.
- Educational lectures and workshops for parents and caregivers on issues related to child safety.

## 1.2 The *Safe Touches* Workshop

The NYSPCC's *Safe Touches* child sexual abuse prevention program is in high demand in New York City. Using appealing, culturally diverse puppets, The NYSPCC clinicians perform skits that help children to recognize sexual abuse and understand what they can do to protect themselves. We use puppets because they can command children's attention and are an effective tool to communicate difficult topics to children: because they are characters, not people, puppets provide an ideal medium for discussing the sensitive issue of child sexual abuse. Puppets engender a world in which children can recognize themselves and identify with the characters, and so once they have entered the world the puppets create, children begin to absorb the key information. Puppets can express what children think and feel, and so children are drawn into the drama but are not threatened by or fearful of it.

Topics covered include how to recognize the differences between safe and not safe touches, what to do if they ever feel at risk, and how to identify whom to tell if they ever experience a not safe touch. We also use the puppets to explain that abuse is never a child's fault and that most of the adults in their lives will protect them. The children play an active role during the workshop by offering suggestions to the puppets about actions they can take to keep their bodies safe and whom they can go to for help if they have been in a not safe situation. Children are also encouraged to ask questions and voice concerns. In fact, each workshop concludes with a discussion period, giving children the opportunity to make comments and ask questions.

The NYSPCC offers the *Safe Touches* program throughout New York City. To date, we have reached approximately 22,000 children (Fig. 1.1).

**Fig. 1.1** The puppets

## *1.2.1  Key Learning Concepts*

Key concepts covered in the workshop include the private parts of the body, the difference between safe and not safe touches, secrets versus surprises, and the ideas that not safe touches can be given by someone the child knows, the child should keep telling an adult until believed, and the child is not to blame for receiving a not safe touch. We also reinforce that not safe touches can happen to boys as well as girls. Facilitators guide the children in making a list of what to do if they experience a not safe touch, as well as in practicing the assertive language skills needed to express discomfort, and how to tell a trusted adult if they have received a not safe touch. The clinicians help the children to make a list of adults that they can tell and emphasize that the children must keep telling until they are believed, as the first person they tell may not be listening or may not believe them.

We use posters of children in bathing suits to help the children to identify what parts of the body are private.

The following is a scene from our train the trainers curriculum where children learn the private parts of their body. We emphasize that they should trust their feelings and, if a touch makes them feel confused, "icky," scared, sad, or just uncomfortable, that they need to act on it and tell an adult.

**Private Parts Script**
**Characters: Facilitators A and B**

*(Facilitator A and B speak directly to the children. Only posters are used in this scene.)*

   **Facilitator A:**

One thing that makes us special is that we all own our bodies. Your body is your own special property. No one should touch you on the private parts of your body or ask you to touch them on their private parts in a way that makes you feel not safe, funny, or confused on the inside.

The private parts are the parts of our body that are covered by a bathing suit.

Let's play a guessing game to see if you can identify the private parts of the body on these posters we have brought with us.

*(Facilitators take out posters of a girl and boy dressed in bathing suits.)* Now, let's play the game!

**Facilitator B:**

Is the hair a private part? No. Can you tell me why?

Is between the legs a private part? Yes. Can you tell me why?

Is the chest a private part? *(The chest may be confusing for the children as the answer is different for boys and girls. If it is causing confusion, hold the posters separately, first asking about the girl and then the boy.)* Even though the chest is not a private part for boys, your body is your own private property and you get to decide what is comfortable for you.

Is your foot a private part? No.

Let's try one more; is the bottom a private part? Yes.

Remember, no one should touch you on the private parts of your body. It can make you feel not safe, funny, or confused inside.

## 1.3  National Institutes of Health Research Study on *Safe Touches*

I applied for an NIH grant because, like most social workers in the child protection field, I have witnessed firsthand the devastation caused by child sexual abuse. As the head of a child advocacy center in the Bronx of New York City during the 1990s, I promoted workshops using puppets, coloring books, and skits to help arm children with knowledge that may support them in thwarting a perpetrator of CSA. The schools usually embraced these workshops, particularly as they were free of charge, conducted by clinicians, and helped schools meet the educational curriculum demands of teaching child sexual abuse prevention concepts to children. There was always a nagging question at the back of my mind, though: "Do the children understand and learn the concepts in the curriculum?" At The NYSPCC, I had the opportunity to test whether or not children truly grasped the concepts, and so we applied to the NIH and were able to conduct a randomized control trial in the New York City public schools from 2012 through 2014.

Two articles were recently published on the research, one in the *American Journal of Public Health*, "Knowledge Gains Following a Child Sexual Abuse Prevention Program Among Urban Students: A Cluster-Randomized Evaluation" (Pulido et al., 2015), and one in the *APSAC Advisor*, "*Safe Touches*: A Child Sexual Abuse Prevention Program Offers Promising Results Among Multi-Racial Children" (Pulido, Tully, & Holloway, 2015).

## *1.3.1 Study Significance and Aims*

CSA prevention efforts have largely consisted of school-based programs. Almost 90% of elementary school districts in the United States offer prevention training (Gibson & Leitenberg, 2000) with over 85% having conducted programs in the past year. About two-thirds of American children have had some exposure to these programs. Despite the prevalence of these programs, there is a dearth of rigorous research evaluating their efficacy. While most studies have been limited by a lack of randomization and control groups, the few randomized trials generally found increased knowledge of CSA prevention concepts in children who received interventions (Oldfield, Hays, & Megel, 1996; Tutty, 1997, 2000). Most studies, however, included only White, middle-class children. An international meta-analysis of randomized controlled trials (RCTs), or quasi-RCTs, found that children who participated in a school-based CSA program were seven times more likely to show self-protective behavior in simulated situations than children who did not attend a program (Zwi et al., 2007). Overall, most studies did not adhere to the intent-to-treat principle, failed to account for nonindependence of students within classrooms, and used small samples that were racially homogeneous.

Our goal was to rigorously evaluate the CSA prevention program *Safe Touches: Personal Safety Training for Children* within a lower-income multiracial population using the Children's Knowledge of Abuse Questionnaire (CKAQ) as an outcome measure. We hypothesized that there would be significant changes on the inappropriate touch scale on the CKAQ from pretest to posttest for the intervention group compared to a control group. We built on previous research by using a large, racially and ethnically diverse, low-socioeconomic status (SES) urban sample within the context of a cluster randomized design. We also wanted to test short-term retention of the *Safe Touches* concepts. A final aim was to assess the fidelity of the implementation.

## *1.3.2 Primary Outcome Measure: The Children's Knowledge of Abuse Questionnaire*

The main dependent measure used for evaluation in this study was the Children's Knowledge of Abuse Questionnaire Revision III (Tutty, 1992). The CKAQ is a validated measure of children's knowledge about CSA concepts and prevention skills and is comprised of two subscales: the inappropriate touch scale (ITS), which measures children's recognition of unsafe situations and people, and the appropriate touch scale (ATS), which measures children's recognition of safe situations and people. The measure consists of 33 items scored "true," "false," or "I don't know," with higher scores reflecting greater knowledge. The CKAQ is among the most widely used outcome measures in CSA prevention research and has been used in urban, multicultural samples (Baker, Gleason, Naai, Mitchell, & Trecker, 2013; Daigneault, Hebert, McDuff, & Frappier, 2012).

Examples of the questions that are on the CKAQ are as follows: "You always have to keep secrets"; "It's OK for someone you like to hug you"; "Sometimes it's OK to say 'no' to a grown-up"; and "If someone touches you in a way you don't like, you should tell someone you trust."

Fidelity monitoring tools were created by the research team. Tracking and reporting implementation fidelity is necessary to the integrity of CSA prevention program replication, but it is lacking within the literature. Thus, three checklists were created for this work that included quantitative and qualitative items: the Workshop Implementation Checklist, the Teacher Follow-Up Checklist, and the Data Collection Checklist. The Workshop Implementation Checklist measured fidelity of *Safe Touches* workshop delivery and documented the extent to which all components of the workshop were administered consistently and according to protocol. Assent and CKAQ administration fidelity were tracked using the Data Collection Checklist and were completed by research staff following each CKAQ administration session. The Teacher Follow-Up Checklist was created to track child disclosures, concerning statements, and adverse events occurring subsequent to the day of the *Safe Touches* workshop.

Recruitment for this study took place in public elementary schools in New York City. Schools were eligible for inclusion if 25% or less of the student body were White, if there were two second or third grade classrooms that were not exclusively special education, and if 75% or more of the students received free lunch. Following outreach to 101 eligible schools, 6 schools agreed to participate in the study. A cluster randomized trial design was used, whereby matched pairs of classrooms within schools were stratified according to grade level and then randomly assigned to intervention or control groups within a stratum. Children in these selected classrooms were eligible for participation if they were at least 7 years of age and had not participated in the *Safe Touches* program in the past. Exclusion criteria included any major physical, cognitive, or emotional impairment that would affect the child's ability to participate in the workshop or to respond to the surveys. Of the 890 eligible children (427 second graders and 453 third graders), 528 children returned parental informed consents. Of these, 492 children in 38 classes assented to be in the study. Thus, 492 second and third graders were enrolled and randomly assigned at the class level to either intervention or control groups.

Research activities took place at three separate time points over a 5-week period at each school. A delayed intervention study design allowed for the collection of data from control participants at times analogous to those of the intervention participants. With this approach, all children would receive the benefit of the *Safe Touches* program, which fulfilled the NYC Department of Education mandate that all children receive personal safety training.

Figure 1.2 displays the timeline of how the study was conducted in the school system.

The CKAQ was administered to all students to provide a pretest baseline 1 week prior to the delivery of the *Safe Touches* program. One week after this baseline test,

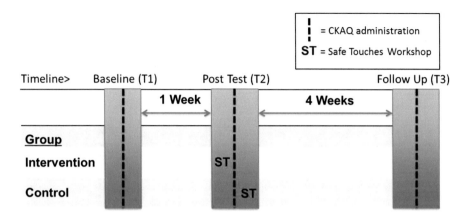

**Fig. 1.2** Study timeline

the clinicians returned to the schools and provided the 50-minute interactive *Safe Touches* workshop for the children in the intervention groups. Meanwhile, children in the control groups participated in their normal classroom activities. At the end of this 50-minute period, all intervention and control group children completed the CKAQ for a second time (posttest 1). At this point, children in the control groups received the *Safe Touches* workshop. Four weeks later, all students completed the CKAQ for a third and final time (posttest 2) to assess for knowledge maintenance.

## *1.3.3  Results*

The overall results of the implementation were decidedly positive. The intervention groups showed significantly greater improvement in knowledge of inappropriate touch than controls at posttest 1. Specifically, intervention group scores on the ITS increased by an average of 1.85 points from baseline to posttest 1. As expected, there was no significant change in ITS scores among children in the control group from baseline to posttest 1. Interestingly, a significant effect was also found in grade levels: intervention group children in second grade demonstrated significantly greater increases in their ITS scores relative to control groups, compared to intervention group children in third grade relative to control (Fig. 1.3).

One month after the children received the workshop, The NYSPCC returned and administered the CKAQ to all participants again. At the 4-week follow-up, children demonstrated retention of significant knowledge gains relative to baseline CKAQ scores (Fig. 1.4).

Teachers and school staff reported overwhelming satisfaction with the program and approval of the delivery of sensitive material and concepts to young children. The majority of children were actively engaged and interested in the presentation and participated in giving feedback to the questions posed by facilitators. Children

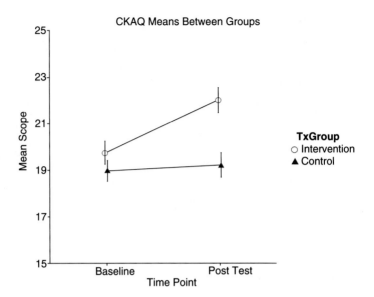

**Fig. 1.3** Mean scores at baseline posttest for children in the intervention ($N = 195$) and control ($N = 242$) groups. At posttest, children in the intervention group had significantly greater CKAQ scores compared to control. (Source: www.nyspcc.org)

readily shouted out answers when given the opportunity, appeared to understand the concepts, and were able to verbalize important points, such as "it's never the child's fault" and "keep telling until someone believes you." Taken together, the study results document the effectiveness and acceptance of *Safe Touches* for use with racially and ethnically diverse groups of children.

## 1.4   The NYSPCC: Building Safe School Communities

In keeping the theme of this conference, I thought it was important to highlight our work in NYC following incidents of child sexual abuse. When there is an incident in the school system, The NYSPCC works with that school to help them put appropriate protocols and training in place to protect children and educate them about child sexual abuse prevention.

### 1.4.1   The NYSPCC Partnership with Horace Mann

The New York Society for the Prevention of Cruelty to Children was engaged by Horace Mann (HM) to provide a range of child protection, education, and review services. Under the partnership, which began in July 2012, The NYSPCC delivered

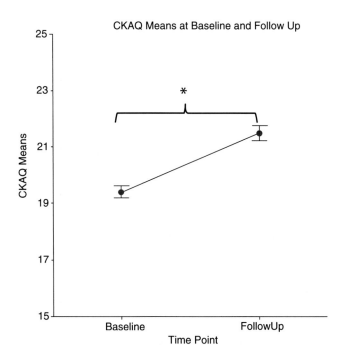

**Fig. 1.4** At a 4-week follow-up, children demonstrated retention of significant knowledge gains relative to baseline CKAQ scores. Mean scores at baseline and follow-up for all children completing both assessments ($N = 411$). *$t(410) = -9.92$, $p < 0.001$. (Source: www.nyspcc.org)

child sexual abuse prevention training for the students; child abuse identification and reporting procedures training for the faculty and staff; and an administrative review and an assessment of current HM policies and procedures regarding child safety and child abuse and neglect reporting. An educational lecture series on topics concerning child abuse prevention and child safety was requested and held for the parents of current HM students. Services provided through The NYSPCC's Training Institute were delivered to HM students, staff, and parents on the HM Riverdale campus or at the Nursery School in Manhattan.

The NYSPCC empathizes deeply with the survivors of past events at the school. The agency's work does not involve that segment of the HM community and that dimension of the situation at the school. Our current work is extensive, but it is limited to the current student body, parents, faculty, and staff regarding events from July 2012 onward.

Working closely with the headmaster of HM, Tom Kelly, PhD, we provided comprehensive support for the school following the press reports of allegations of widespread child sexual abuse that had occurred decades earlier. This included a review of all policies and procedures that impact child safety, providing *Safe Touches* workshops for all children in kindergarten through third grade, CSA prevention training for all children in grades 4 through 12, training in identifying and reporting child abuse and neglect for all faculty and staff, and presentations to the parents, the alumni association, and the board of directors. The NYSPCC has continued to return to campus each year to conduct refresher courses with the current student body, and all new staff take our child abuse identification and reporting course online. The goal is to build a safe school community to prevent child sexual abuse.

### 1.4.2 Curriculum for Students from Kindergarten to the Third Grade

*Safe Touches* was utilized to train students from kindergarten through the third grade. A video from our training curriculum highlights the "four safety tools" that we teach children to protect themselves from unwanted, not safe touches. The children really seem to grasp these concepts. The script from the video follows.

**"The Four Safety Tools"**
*(Facilitator A will play Petunia and Facilitator B will play Uncle Herbert)*

**Facilitator B:** Now we're going to learn four safety tools that you can use to keep your body safe when someone tries to touch you on your private parts or asks you to touch them. Now, I am going to say and show you each of the safety tools, and I want you to repeat after me. Are you ready? Here we go:

1. Trust your feelings. *(Facilitators rub their tummy. Class repeats.)*
2. Try to say no. *(Facilitators put their hand out. Class repeats.)*
3. Try to walk away. *(Facilitators move their arms to gesture walking. Class repeats.)*
4. Tell an adult. *(Facilitators put their hands beside the mouth and move the body forward. Class* repeats.)

Now let's do it one more time! *(Repeat four tools above.)* Now let's watch another show. Watch very closely and remember your safety tools because it will be your job to help keep Petunia safe. Herbert is Petunia's uncle. How old do you think Petunia should be? Think of an age between 5 and 10. Ok, Petunia is ____ (e.g., *6 years old).*

**Petunia:** Hi Uncle Herbert.
**Herbert:** Hey Petunia…why don't you turn off the TV and come sit on my lap; I want to play a game with you.
**Petunia:** Okay, I love games.
**Herbert:** Well, this game is called the love game. I am going to tickle you on your stomach like I always do, and then I am going to put my hand under your shirt and touch your chest. Isn't that nice?
**Petunia:** You want to touch my chest? Umm…I don't know. *(Petunia looks uncomfortable, looks down, and scratches her head.)*
**Herbert:** If you play this game, I will buy you a new iPad!

**Petunia:** A new iPad?

**Herbert:** Yes, but it will be our secret; you can't tell anyone.

**Petunia:** I can't even tell Mommy?

**Herbert:** Not even Mommy…it's our secret. *(Herbert places hand on Petunia's chest.)*

**Facilitator B:** *Freeze…* Wow! How do you think Petunia feels? Do you think she feels sad? Do you think she feels confused? Why does she feel confused? *(Confusion is a common feeling among children who have been sexually abused. In your response, make sure to highlight the confusion children may feel. For example, "That's right, Petunia is probably feeling really confused because she loves her Uncle Herbert, but she does not like what he is doing.")* What kind of a touch do you think that was? Petunia has never heard the safety tools before. Do you think we can teach them to her to help keep her body safe? Now, together let's teach Petunia the safety tools. Are you ready?

1. Trust your feelings. *(Facilitators rub their tummy. Class repeats.)*
2. Try to say no. *(Facilitators put their hand out. Class repeats.)*
3. Try to walk away. *(Facilitators move their arms to gesture walking. Class repeats.)*
4. Tell an adult. *(Facilitators put their hands beside mouth and move body forward. Class repeats.)*

**Facilitator B:** Thank you for helping to teach Petunia the safety tools! Now that Petunia knows all the things that she can do to keep her body safe, let's see if she can use these safety tools to help keep her body safe. Let's see what happens when we do the scene again…

**Petunia:** Thanks class. Now I remember my safety tools. *(Herbert reappears.)*

**Herbert:** Well, this game is called the love game. I am going to tickle you on your stomach like I always do, and then I am going to put my hand under your shirt and touch your chest. Isn't that nice?

**Petunia:** You want to touch my chest? Umm…I don't know.

**Herbert:** If you play this game, I will buy you a new iPad!

**Petunia:** A new iPad?

**Herbert:** Yes, but it will be our secret, you can't tell anyone.

**Petunia:** I can't even tell Mommy?

**Herbert:** Not even Mommy…it's our secret. *(Places hand on Petunia's chest.)*

**Petunia:** Hmm… I have a funny feeling in my tummy. I'm feeling scared, confused, and not safe. I'm going to trust my feelings! No! I don't want to play that game! I'm going to "walk away" to my room now. I'm going to tell my Mommy and Daddy about this when they get home.

**Facilitator B:** Wow nice job you guys, you taught Petunia all four safety tools and she was able to keep her body safe! Remember that sometimes you may like or love the person, but you may not like the touch.

### 1.4.3 Curriculum for Children in the Fourth and Fifth Grade

The children at this age may be too old to be captivated by puppet shows, so an interactive, 50-minute workshop was developed for fourth and fifth graders that uses videos, presentation, and group discussion to engage children in learning about child sexual abuse, safe and not safe touches, issues surrounding secrecy, what to do and whom to tell if a child receives a not safe touch, and how they can keep their bodies safe. In one exercise, entitled "What If?," children are asked questions by the facilitators to see if they would know what to do in questionable situations. Examples include "What if a neighbor asks you to come to his house for a cookie, but tells you not to tell your parents?" and "What if your teacher/uncle/priest gives you a not safe touch? Whom would you tell?"

### 1.4.4 Curriculum for Children in the Middle Division, Grades 6–8

For the middle division, two teaching formats were used. A 1-hour didactic lecture was held with each grade separately, and then the children were organized into smaller groups of 20–25 where this information could be processed and questions answered. The group lecture included video clips and covered facts and statistics on child sexual abuse, power dynamics, stages of the grooming process, reasons why youth might not disclose child sexual abuse, and the importance of telling an adult if it does happen. In the breakout groups, one of the activities was a "myth versus fact" activity that reinforced the key points of the lecture. Interestingly, the issue of "stranger danger" was a regular discussion item: students were surprised to learn that 90 percent of child sexual abuse is committed by someone the child knows and trusts.

### 1.4.5 Curriculum for Youth in the Upper Division, Grades 9–12

A similar format was used for the upper division, grades 9–12, with a 1-hour didactic lecture and then small breakout groups for 50 minutes. A variety of activities, vignettes, videos, contemporary media, and reflection tools were utilized. The high school students learned facts and statistics on victims and perpetrators, definitions of abuse, the cycle of abuse, and understanding why survivors of abuse often stay silent. Grooming techniques of perpetrators were discussed, as were the reasons why teens may have trouble saying "no" or getting out of inappropriate or nonconsensual sexual relationships with adults. The issue of legal consent comes up regularly when dealing with teens, especially in the context of consent with each other.

We use a video by Emmeline May and the Blue Seat Studios (2015) entitled "Consent—It's Simple as Tea" as a conversation starter on this topic with the high school students.

Our partnership with HM includes annual training for the students and staff. As a way of giving back to the Bronx community, HM provides funding for The NYSPCC to deliver *Safe Touches* workshops to students from kindergarten through the third grade in the Bronx public school system. We reach approximately 3500 children a year.

## 1.5  *Safe Touches* Collaboration with the Country of Greece

The NYSPCC has partnered with the ELIZA Society for the Prevention of Cruelty to Children to support the development of a groundbreaking child sexual abuse prevention program in Greece. This work, which targets children from ages 5 through 9, is based on The NYSPCC's *Safe Touches* program; it will first be implemented in Athens schools and ultimately expanded to more rural and remote Greek island locations. Work will be executed in three phases, with Phase I focusing on the adaptation of The NYSPCC's *Safe Touches* program materials, training, and consultation for ELIZA staff and the initiation of a pilot study with kindergarten-aged children in Athens. Phases II and III will focus on expanding and scaling the intervention, data collection, and research dissemination.

This collaborative project stands at the forefront of child sexual abuse prevention work in Greece and will help to address a serious unmet need for education and awareness. According to ELIZA, one in six children in Greece is the victim of at least one incident of sexual abuse during childhood, and Greece's systems and infrastructure to support victims of abuse are virtually nonexistent. There is a lack of primary sexual abuse prevention programs, no national registry for the reporting and recording of sexual abuse cases, and services for victims of abuse are limited, making intervention and prevention efforts even more challenging. This innovative partnership, funded by the Stavros Niarchos Foundation, is a huge step forward for child protection efforts in Greece, increasing awareness and education around child sexual abuse.

In April 2016, The NYSPCC traveled to Greece to conduct a "train the trainers" session with 20 psychologists and their interns on *Safe Touches*. The Greek Ministry of Education recently approved their request to launch *Safe Touches* in the public school system. ELIZA will also be conducting a research study using the CKAQ. Having translated the CKAQ into Greek, a pilot has already begun, and in May and June of 2016, 200 children in the kindergarten and the first grade were enrolled. ELIZA has conducted a preliminary data analysis and found that first graders are showing an increase in knowledge from pre- to posttest. The group plans to enroll 500 more children by the end of fall 2016 and has also translated the take-home children's book *My Body Belongs to Me* into Greek, so that the parents could reinforce the concepts learned in the workshop with their children (Fig. 1.5).

**Fig. 1.5** Take-home activity booklets

Throughout Phase I and the remainder of the project, The NYSPCC will serve as advisors, supporting and providing the ELIZA team with programmatic, clinical, research, and advocacy consultation as they adapt and pilot *Safe Touches* in Greece.

The NYSPCC's next step is to obtain another research grant for *Safe Touches*. The NIH study showed that children understand the concepts and retain them in the short term; we plan to apply for funding for longitudinal studies to see if that translates into behavioral changes. We are also completing "train the trainers" instructional kits for the other child sexual abuse prevention modules for children in grades 4–12. We would also like to obtain funding to produce web-based applications for CSA prevention to reach even more children and parents.

In closing, I would like to thank Jennie Noll and the Pennsylvania State University for this opportunity and for your leadership in protecting children throughout the country.

# References

Baker, C. K., Gleason, K., Naai, R., Mitchell, J., & Trecker, C. (2013). Increasing knowledge of sexual abuse: A study with elementary school children in Hawaii. *Research on Social Work Practice, 23*(2), 167–178.

Daigneault, I., Hebert, M., McDuff, P., & Frappier, J. (2012). Evaluation of a sexual abuse prevention workshop in a multicultural, impoverished urban area. *Journal of Child Sexual Abuse, 21*(5), 521–542.

Finkelhor, D. (1990). Early and long term effects of child sexual abuse: An update: A review and recommendations. *Journal of the American Academy of Child and Adolescent Psychiatry, 34*(11), 1408–1423.

Finkelhor, D. (1994). Current information on the scope and nature of child sexual abuse. *The Future of Children, 4*(2), 31–53. https://doi.org/10.2307/1602522

Gibson, L., & Leitenberg, H. (2000). Child sexual abuse prevention programs: Do they decrease the occurrence of child sexual abuse? *Child Abuse and Neglect, 24*(9), 1115–1125.

Neumann, D. A., Houskamp, B. M., Pollock, V. E., & Briere, J. (1996). The long-term sequelae of childhood sexual abuse in women: A meta-analytic review. *Child Maltreatment, 1*, 6–16.

Noll, J. G., Zeller, M. H., Trickett, P. K., & Putnam, F. W. (2007). Obesity risk for female victims of childhood sexual abuse: A prospective study. *Pediatrics, 120*, e61–e67. https://doi.org/10.1542/peds.2006-3058

Oldfield, D., Hays, B. J., & Megel, M. E. (1996). Evaluation of the effectiveness of Project Trust: An elementary school-based victimization prevention strategy. *Child Abuse and Neglect, 20*(9), (9), 821–832.

Pulido, M. L., Dauber, S., Tully, B., Hamilton, P., Smith, M., & Freeman, K. (2015). Knowledge gains following a child sexual abuse prevention program among urban students: A cluster-randomized evaluation. *American Journal of Public Health, 105*(7), 1334–1350.

Pulido, M. L., Tully, B., & Holloway, J. (2015). Safe Touches: A child sexual abuse prevention program offers promising results among multi-racial children. *American Professional Society on the Abuse of Children (APSAC) Advisor, 27*(1), 1–8.

Putnam, F. W. (2003). Ten-year research update review: Child sexual abuse. *Journal of the American Academy of Child & Adolescent Psychiatry, 42*(2), 269–278.

Tutty, L. (1992). The ability of elementary school children to learn child sexual abuse prevention concepts. *Child Abuse and Neglect, 16*, 369–384.

Tutty, L. (1997). Child sexual abuse prevention programs: Evaluating Who Do You Tell. *Child Abuse and Neglect, 21*(9), 869–881.

Tutty, L. (2000). What children learn from sexual abuse prevention programs: Difficult concepts and developmental issues. *Research on Social Work Practice, 10*(3), 275–300.

Zwi, K., Woolfenden, S., Wheeler, D. M., O'Brien, T., Tait, P., & Williams, K. J. (2007). School-based education programs for the prevention of child sexual abuse. *The Cochrane Database of Systematic Reviews*, 1–4.

# Chapter 2
# The Fourth R: Teaching Healthy Relationship Skills to Reduce Youth Risk Behaviors

**Claire V. Crooks and David A. Wolfe**

## 2.1 Introduction

Most parents can agree on critical goals for their children as they grow into adolescence and young adulthood. First and foremost, we want them to be safe from harm. We don't want people to hurt them, and we don't want them to hurt other people. We want them to experience happiness, and we want them to get through high school without addictions, pregnancies, injuries, or violence. Increasingly, we expect educators to play a major role in preparing youth for adulthood, yet that begs the question: what tools are we giving educators to do so?

The Fourth R curriculum was developed for schools to help youth navigate the perils of adolescence while addressing the fears of parents that their children could be victimized, harmed, or take part in behaviors that carry significant risk. Starting with age-appropriate curricula that help youths develop healthy relationships skills and reduce risk behaviors, the Fourth R curriculum is well-suited to protect them from the increasing dangers related to sex, drugs, and violence. Importantly, the curriculum provides educators with the tools needed to address the concerns that parents have about bullying, homophobia, drugs, alcohol, promiscuity, and mental illness, among other subjects. It is hard to argue that implementation of a curriculum teaching the basic skills of relationships and respect could be a bad thing for children and youth. To the contrary, such lessons would have a positive, long-lasting benefit.

Getting it right from the start leads to better outcomes and is less costly than trying to fix it later. With this vision parents and educators can embrace creative

C. V. Crooks (✉)
Faculty of Education, Centre for School Mental Health, Western University,
London, ON, Canada
e-mail: ccrooks@uwo.ca

D. A. Wolfe
Faculty of Education, Western Univeristy, London, ON, Canada

© Springer Nature Switzerland AG 2019
C. C. Panlilio (ed.), *Trauma-Informed Schools*, Child Maltreatment Solutions
Network, https://doi.org/10.1007/978-3-030-12811-1_2

strategies that reduce harm, foster healthy relationships, and maximize a successful transition to adulthood. Far from causing children and youth to develop behaviors that parents do not want, the Fourth R demystifies the causes of unwanted behaviors and provides skills to prepare youth to make safe and healthier choices. In this chapter we outline how this program was developed to address the *relational* needs of youth and discuss the practical strategies available to implementing the Fourth R in conjunction with federal, state, and provincial educational requirements.

## 2.1.1   The Relationship Connection

Physical abuse, sexual abuse, elder abuse, dating violence, sexual assault, and many other forms of violence are connected by one very important element: relationships. Most significantly, these forms of abuse and violence are highly preventable. Approaches to reducing any of these forms of violence have much greater impact when they focus on the risk and protective factors leading to violence, rather than trying to "treat" violence after the fact. All children need some inoculation around the topic of healthy and unhealthy relationships; because these issues are connected by their relationship context, it is not sufficient to teach them about bullying, sexual abuse, or dating violence alone. Schools can build healthy relationships—and reduce unhealthy ones—by addressing the underlying common elements affecting abuse and trauma.

Education is arguably the biggest key in terms of preventing relational violence and trauma. In particular, we have argued that early to mid-adolescence is perhaps our best window of opportunity (Wolfe, Jaffe, & Crooks, 2006). Adolescence is a time of autonomy, transition, and experimentation. A key challenge for youth is to develop autonomy, which often translates into breaking away from parental oversight and values and matching more closely to those of their peer group. Notably, the relationship skills they form in early and middle childhood carry forward into their future relationships. As they experiment with new opportunities and privileges in adolescence, their prior relationships can be protective or create new risks.

## 2.2   What Is the Fourth R?

The Fourth R is a range of healthy relationship programs developed for school and community settings. It is based on the contention that relationship skills can be taught in the same way as many other academic or athletic skills, through breaking down the steps and giving youth lots of guided practice. The programs were developed over the last 20 years by a consortium of researchers, educators, and psychologists at the University of Western Ontario and the Centre for Addiction and Mental Health (CAMH) Centre for Prevention Science in London, Ontario. Today, there are Fourth R versions available that align with curriculum expectations for all Canadian provinces and US states to minimize barriers to implementation. In addition to the original Grade 9 physical health and education curriculum, the Fourth R offers healthy living curricula for seventh through ninth grades and English curricula for ninth through 12th grades.

There are additional versions of the Fourth R that have been developed for different First Nations perspectives, as well as for alternative education settings. Most recently, a version for small groups was developed called the Healthy Relationships Plus Program (Exner-Cortens, Wolfe, Crooks, & Chiodo, 2019; Lapshina, Crooks, & Kerry, 2018). We have further developed healthy relationships programs for specific groups of vulnerable youth, including LGBT2Q+ youth (Lapointe & Crooks, 2018). Some components of the program have also been translated into French, Spanish, Portuguese, and Polish to meet the needs of various communities. There are also teacher training options, including opportunities to become master trainers.

## 2.2.1  Guiding Principles of the Fourth R

### 2.2.1.1  Universal Focus

As part of their K-12 education, all students are taught to read. Similarly, all students should have opportunities to learn healthy relationship skills and other social and emotional learning (SEL) competencies (Greenberg et al., 2003). We can build resilience for future challenges when we include all adolescents, rather than just those who show problems, in education about how to develop healthy relationships and avoid risk behaviors. A universal approach precludes the need to target programs to particular youth and reduces the stigma of labeling youth as high risk.

### 2.2.1.2  Positive Youth Development

In the past, health education has emphasized negative behaviors that youth should avoid but omitted discussion of the assets that youth can build. The Fourth R focuses on positive youth development, going beyond avoiding negative outcomes to focus on building strong core capacities among adolescents (Catalano, Berglund, Ryan, Lonczak, & Hawkins, 2004). In the field of education, an emphasis on SEL has emerged, emphasizing the processes through which children and adults attain core capacities that are critical to positive development. The five SEL competency domains, as defined by the Collaborative for Academic, Social, and Emotional Learning (CASEL), are self-awareness, self-management, social awareness, relationship skills, and responsible decision-making. Thus, SEL encapsulates the processes through which children and adults acquire and effectively apply the knowledge, attitudes, and skills necessary to understand and manage emotions, set and achieve positive goals, feel and show empathy for others, establish and maintain positive relationships, and make responsible decisions (Collaborative for Academic, Social, and Emotional Learning, 2013). Students who have strong social and emotional skills have more positive relationships with peers and adults and have more positive emotional adjustment and mental health, both as children and into adulthood (Domitrovich, Durlak, Staley, & Weissberg, 2017). Students in schools that implement specific SEL programs also perform better academically than their peers in schools without such programs (Durlak, Weissberg, Dymnicki, Taylor, & Schellinger, 2011). Furthermore, the positive impacts of these social and emotional competencies are long-lasting, as demonstrated in a recent meta-analysis looking at long-term effects up to 18 years post-intervention (Taylor, Oberle, Durlak, & Weissberg, 2017).

### 2.2.1.3 Skills-Based Approach

The contention of the Fourth R is that relationship skills can be taught in the same way as many other academic or athletic skills, through breaking down the steps and giving youths lots of guided practice. A skills-based approach is one component of effective programming in general, and programs often use role-plays to build skills. However, role plays can be difficult to implement effectively due to an educator's own confidence level or perception of how receptive students will be to role play activities. To address these concerns, the Fourth R has developed and refined an incremental approach to role plays in order to support educators and students in creating a successful experience. The Fourth R has also developed additional training supports regarding role plays.

### 2.2.1.4 Relationships Are the Core Foundation

Finally, the Fourth R is based on the premise that healthy relationships are a key context for understanding the risk behaviors that are a central focus of the program (i.e., violence, substance use, and sexual behavior). It is our premise that, first and foremost, students should be taught ways to build healthy relationships and interpersonal strengths, rather than ways to avoid particular problem behaviors alone. For example, for decades, educators (and parents!) have targeted unwanted youth risk behaviors one at a time (e.g., alcohol or drug abuse; bullying; sexual relationships), overlooking the overlap and relationship context of risk behaviors.

As shown in Fig. 2.1, relationships provide the core context for other behavior areas, both as risk factors—unhealthy peer and family relationships can increase the likelihood of engaging in risk behaviors—and, conversely, as protective factors: healthy, positive relationships can prevent the development of risk behaviors. Focusing on relationships has the added benefit of being highly engaging for youths, as it mirrors the contexts that matter in their social world. The ultimate goal of Fourth R programs is to help youths develop the social and emotional competencies they will need to make safe choices and avoid the "triad" of risk behaviors: violence, unsafe sexual behavior, and substance misuse. Although the Fourth R was originally developed to address the triad of risk behaviors within the context of relationships (Wolfe et al., 2006), over the past decade, we have increasingly integrated mental

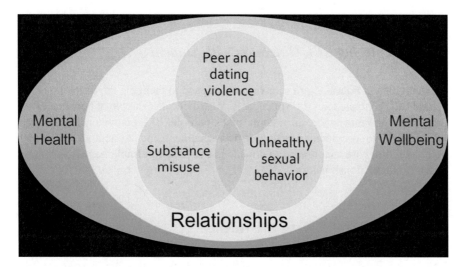

**Fig. 2.1** Relationships as the context for co-occurring risk behaviors among adolescents

health promotion into all Fourth R programs to address the connections among relationships, mental health, and risk factors.

### 2.2.2   What Do Fourth R Programs Look Like?

The Fourth R was designed to be taught by classroom teachers and is aligned with state and provincial health curricula for Grades 7, 8, and 9. For example, the core components of the Grade 9 healthy living curriculum are covered in four units: (1) personal safety and injury prevention, (2) healthy growth and sexuality, (3) substance use and abuse, and (4) healthy eating. The Fourth R includes a detailed lesson plan for each unit. A wide variety of interactive teaching strategies is used to cover topics within these units, to engage youths and help them develop critical thinking skills. The healthy eating activities are designed to be integrated into other physical education activities rather than in the classroom. Teacher training is available in person or online and provides important background, implementation considerations, orientation to the program materials, and extensive skill practice.

The Fourth R lessons and units are taught in sequence, with each lesson building upon the skills presented in earlier lessons. Whenever possible, every lesson in Units 1 through 4 should be covered; if this is not possible, we strongly recommend that at least 80% of the material be covered. All lessons start with an introductory activity and end with an exit statement or activity. Each lesson plan includes specific expectations for the lesson aligned to state or provincial expectations; a list of required materials; teaching and learning strategies; suggestions for how to facilitate the lesson; and teaching options, such as activities with different options to be selected from to best meet the needs of the students.

### 2.2.3  Achieving SEL Outcomes with Students

The activities in Fourth R programs were designed to facilitate the development of certain SEL competencies. In Appendix A we provide an example of how one of our programs, the ninth grade curriculum, maps onto the SEL competencies. Readers interested in a more detailed listing of how specific curricular activities map onto youth outcomes are encouraged to download our Fourth R Implementation Manual (www.youthrelationships.org).

## 2.3  Overview of Fourth R Evidence

The Fourth R team has published several studies evaluating the program and its implementation. Some of these were conducted within the context of two randomized controlled trials (RCTs), whereas others used different methodologies. Highlights are summarized below.

### 2.3.1  Grade 9 Program Reduces Dating Violence, Increases Condom Use

This study utilized a cluster RCT design (Wolfe et al., 2009), which assigned schools (clusters) to the intervention or control condition. The intervention condition was the Fourth R Grade 9 health and physical education program, a 21-lesson curriculum delivered during 28 hours by teachers with additional training in the dynamics of dating violence and healthy relationships. Control schools targeted similar objectives without the training or materials using standard teaching methods. Over 1700 students aged 14 to 15 years participated in this study (total sample size = 1722); these students were surveyed before receiving programming and 2.5 years after the program. Results indicated that physical dating violence was about 2.5 times greater among control versus intervention students at the date of follow-up. The Fourth R intervention had a stronger impact on reducing physical dating violence among boys than girls. The Fourth R intervention also improved condom use in sexually active boys when compared to their counterparts in the control condition.

## 2.3.2 A Buffering Impact Against Violent Delinquency Among Maltreated Youth

Child maltreatment (including different types of abuse, neglect, and exposure to family violence) constitutes a significant risk for adolescent delinquency. We used data from our first randomized controlled trial to look at predictors of violent delinquency, both at the individual and the school level (Crooks, Scott, Wolfe, Chiodo, & Killip, 2007). Results at the individual level identified being male, experiencing maltreatment in childhood, and having poor parental nurturing as important predictors of violent delinquency. Maltreatment in particular was a very strong predictor, and cumulative experiences of maltreatment led to a greatly increased risk. At the school level, school climate also played a significant role in predicting delinquency: schools where students felt safer had fewer ninth grade students engaging in violent delinquent behaviors. Finally, the impact of childhood maltreatment on risk of engaging in violent delinquency was greater among those schools that had not participated in the Fourth R. Thus, youths with the same risk factors had a lower likelihood of engaging in violent delinquency if they were at a Fourth R school, compared to a school that did not offer the program. These results highlight the protective impact a school-based healthy relationship program can have for vulnerable youth. Furthermore, this protective impact was still evident 2 years after the intervention (Crooks, Scott, Ellis, & Wolfe, 2011).

## 2.3.3 Better Peer Resistance and Communication Skills

Because the Fourth R focuses on developing skills and not merely avoiding negative outcomes, we have investigated the skill acquisition process by examining peer resistance skills following the Grade 9 Fourth R program (Wolfe, Crooks, Chiodo, Hughes, & Ellis, 2012). Observational data from 196 ninth grade students participating in the cluster RCT (98 treatment, 98 control) were used to evaluate post-intervention acquisition of peer resistance skills. Pairs of students engaged in a role play paradigm with older student actors, wherein they were subjected to increasing pressure to comply with peer requests related to drugs and alcohol, bullying, and sexual behavior. Videotaped role plays were coded by two different sets of blinded coders: research assistants who coded five specific behavioral responses (negotiation, delay, yielding to pressure, refusal, and compliance) and teachers who rated the observations on four global indices (thinking and inquiry, application, communication, and perceived efficacy). As predicted, Fourth R students were more likely to demonstrate negotiation skills and less likely to yield to negative pressure relative to controls. Intervention girls were much more likely to use delay than control girls, who were more likely to use refusal. The number of times treatment students complied with peer requests did not differ from the control group. Teacher ratings showed Fourth R youth to be more competent across all domains.

## 2.3.4 Significant Cost Savings

Finally, we have conducted some economic cost/benefit analysis regarding the Fourth R. We calculated costs for four different implementation scenarios, showing that even at its most expensive form of delivery, the program costs $33/person (Crooks et al., 2017). Significant costs are averted due to reduced violence perpetration, confirming that the Fourth R is a strong component of a public health approach to reducing youth violence.

## 2.3.5 Additional Information

The Fourth R Grade 9 program has undergone extensive review by a number of the organizations that certify approaches as best practice based on rigorous research. Based on such reviews, the Fourth R has been categorized as a model/best or promising practice by the following organizations:

- US Office of Juvenile Justice and Delinquency Prevention's Model Programs Guide: http://www.ojjdp.gov/mpg/
- US Department of Justice's Office of Justice Programs (OJP): www.crimesolutions.gov
- Public Health Agency of Canada Best Practices Portal: http://cbpp-pcpe.phac-aspc.gc.ca/intervention/617/view-eng.html
- Public Safety Canada Promising and Model Crime Prevention Programs: http://www.publicsafety.gc.ca/res/cp/res/2011-pcpp-eng.aspx#toc_4d
- NREPP: SAMHSA's National Registry of Evidence-based Programs and Practices: http://nrepp.samhsa.gov/ViewIntervention.aspx?id=207
- CASEL: Collaborative for Academic, Social, and Emotional Learning: http://secondaryguide.casel.org/

## 2.4 Implementation Overview

Implementing the Fourth R can begin in a variety of ways and at different levels of the school system, but there are certain key steps that are common to all strong implementation processes. First, someone within the school system needs to have a reasonably strong understanding of the Fourth R—what it is, how it works, and what teachers can expect for themselves and their students—in order to decide to adopt the program (or recommend it for adoption). After the decision is made to implement the program and the adoption phase begins, readiness is built, and educators are trained. Third, the program is implemented. Afterward, issues of sustainability are addressed, and this is followed by feedback and evaluation to inform future cycles.

## 2.4.1   Importance of Implementation Quality

A rigorously evaluated evidence-based program may not produce the desired outcomes unless it is implemented properly. Implementation quality or fidelity refers to a program being implemented the way it was designed to be implemented and found to be effective. Having good implementation quality does not imply a one-size-fits-all approach or that there is no flexibility to meet the needs of a particular group of learners. Instead, it means that the core of the program is maintained, especially the parts that are responsible for creating change.

### 2.4.1.1   Good implementation of the Fourth R includes

- Implementation by teachers who have received training in the Fourth R, rather than teachers trying to utilize new strategies and role play approaches without preparation.
- Ensuring that enough of the program is delivered (i.e., dosage), rather than shortening the classes or dropping sessions all together.
- Using the strategies in the program, rather than replacing the interactive activities and role plays with didactic methods.
- Ensuring that the role plays are taught and debriefed properly, rather than being done in a haphazard way or not at all.
- Teaching the program in sequence so that the skill building happens in a thoughtful and incremental manner, rather than jumping around in the program.
- Ensuring that the classroom setup and teaching style are consistent with the program objectives, rather than utilizing Fourth R materials but maintaining a teacher-centered lecture style with an emphasis on maintaining authority.
- Undertaking proactive adaptation to meet students' needs, rather than reactive adaptation. (Guidelines for appropriate adaptations are available in our implementation manual with the use of red, yellow, and green light traffic signal guidance.)

There are additional important considerations for implementing Fourth R programs with diverse youth or in particular settings (see Crooks, Chiodo, Dunlop, Lapointe, & Kerry, 2018).

## 2.5   Final Thoughts

Universal prevention studies indicate that effective programs deliver the proper dosage of information and skills, are well-timed to student needs, are delivered properly, and offer appropriate content in the best setting (Nation et al., 2003). Educational and therapeutic programs, in other words, need to be well-timed and well-matched to their intended age group and population. The Fourth R program was established on the principle that all youths need education about healthy, non-violent relationships and accurate information delivered in a positive fashion without scare tactics. Youths also need personal value clarification and education on personal limits and boundary setting. The education system is ideally suited to provide such opportunities while minimizing stigma and exclusion.

The Fourth R program was designed to help youth strengthen relationship skills and assist them in making safe and responsible choices. By integrating the lessons into standard curriculum requirements, the program aims to provide all youths with the basic skills and knowledge to advance their goals and reduce their involvement in risk behaviors. We want youths to talk about the challenges they face and the solutions they are seeking, to be honest about these challenges, and to seek advice from trusted adults. We want youths to feel responsibility and be committed to achieving healthy relationships, rather than fall prey to the omnipresent pressures from their social worlds to experiment prematurely with adult privileges like sex and alcohol use. We want to counteract pro-abuse messages—negative messages based on gender, race, sexual orientation, and so forth—that youth experience on a regular basis. We want youths to have the skills and the sense of personal responsibility to assist struggling peers. Most of all, we want to provide youth with positive messages of safety and harm reduction, rather than scare tactics that do little to prepare them.

Looking into the future, our team is focusing on two research directions. First, we are examining the ingredients necessary for successful implementation, scale, and sustainability of Fourth R programming. To live up to the promise of embedding a public health approach to violence prevention in schools, we need to better understand how to support implementation and sustainability. Second, we are exploring how to adapt programming to meet the needs of more vulnerable or high-risk youth in complex settings. To that end we are currently piloting an enhanced version of Healthy Relationships Plus in several youth justice and community mental health settings, and we are evaluating our program that was designed to meet the needs of LGBT2Q+ youth. Ultimately, we have a vision of well-designed, evidence-informed programs with strong implementation supports that ensure all youths have the opportunity to develop healthy relationships skills.

We encourage interested readers to visit our website (www.youthrelationships. org) to see the full range of Fourth R programs, training, and support.

# Appendix A

Fourth R Activities Designed to Meet Social and Emotional Learning Outcomes (SEL)

| SEL outcome domain | Fourth R program connections |
|---|---|
| Sense of belonging | Resilience (balloons)<br>Thinking about influences (stand on the line)<br>Message of hope (commemorative tile)<br>Support |
| Self-awareness | Holistic view of health<br>Strategies for safe use of technology<br>Mindfulness<br>Understanding conflict (fold the line)<br>Self-regulation (carousel)<br>Dealing with anger<br>Assertive skills for conflict resolution (role play)<br>Assertive communication when conflict escalates (role play)<br>Coping when a relationship ends<br>Rights/responsibilities when a relationship/friendship ends<br>Resilience<br>What's in our control<br>Consent<br>Sexuality rights and responsibilities<br>Delay, negotiation, refusal skills (role play)<br>Setting goals and priorities<br>Preventing unintended pregnancy and STIs<br>Tracking food, exercise, and sleep<br>SMART goal setting<br>Skills to resist influences related to food and beverage choices |
| Self-management | My health (synectics)<br>Recognizing stressors (jigsaw)<br>Personal technology use<br>Recognizing warning signs/symptoms related to mental health<br>Knowing when to seek adult help<br>Preventing and responding to harmful behaviors<br>Understanding consent<br>Protective and risk factors (inside/outside circle)<br>What's in our control<br>Influences, consequences, and protective factors to binge drinking<br>Social influence/pressure<br>Skills/strategies to build healthy social and intimate relationships (graffiti)<br>What creates a sense of self<br>There's nobody like me<br>Being yourself<br>Factors that influence understanding of gender identity and sexual orientation<br>Sexuality rights and responsibilities |

| SEL outcome domain | Fourth R program connections |
|---|---|
| Social awareness | Considering stressors |
| | Stress as a part of life |
| | Peer safety action plan |
| | Avoiding communication barriers |
| | Recognizing warning signs/symptoms related to mental health |
| | Peer and dating relationships |
| | Understanding conflict (fold the line) |
| | Anger situations |
| | Preventing and responding to harmful behaviors |
| | Warning signs of an unhealthy or abusive relationship |
| | Understanding consent |
| | Protective and risk factors (inside/outside circle) |
| | Influences on substance use and other problematic behaviors (communication line) |
| | Current use/abuse and addictive behaviors |
| | Transforming the legacy of residential schools |
| | Influences, consequences, and protective factors to binge drinking |
| | Social influence/pressure |
| | Skills/strategies to build healthy social and intimate relationships (graffiti) |
| | Factors that influence understanding of gender identity and sexual orientation |
| | Media influences |
| | Assumptions about masculinity, femininity, and relationships |
| | Sexuality rights and responsibilities |
| | Social and environmental influences on food choices |
| Relationship skills | Avoiding communication barriers |
| | Reflecting feelings (role play) |
| | Practicing help seeking and support (role play) |
| | Peer and dating relationships |
| | Understanding assertive, passive, and aggressive communication styles |
| | Assertive communication (role play) |
| | Assertive skills for conflict resolution (role play) |
| | Assertive communication when conflict escalates (role play) |
| | Verbal apology (role play) |
| | Warning signs of an unhealthy or abusive relationship |
| | Understanding consent |
| | Rights/responsibilities when a relationship/friendship ends |
| | Respectfully ending a relationship (role play) |
| | Delay, negotiation, refusal skills (role play) |
| | Skills/strategies to build healthy social and intimate relationships (graffiti) |
| | Preventing unintended pregnancy and STIs |
| | Factors to consider about sexual relationships |
| | Deciding if consent was given |
| | Sexuality rights and responsibilities |
| | Defining sexual violence |
| | Consequences of sexual assault |

| SEL outcome domain | Fourth R program connections |
|---|---|
| Responsible decision-making | Benefits and risks of electronic communication |
| | Strategies for safe use of technology |
| | Communication technology mantra |
| | Knowing when to seek adult help |
| | Understanding consent |
| | Influences on substance use and other problematic behaviors (communication line) |
| | Consequences to substance use and other addictive behaviors |
| | Consequences of binge drinking |
| | Consent |
| | IDEAL decision-making |
| | Setting goals and priorities |
| | STIs information and review |
| | Preventing unintended pregnancy and STIs |
| | Factors to consider about sexual relationships |
| | Deciding if consent was given |
| | Defining sexual violence |
| Skill building and help-seeking strategies | Coping skills (rules of five) |
| | Mindfulness |
| | Avoiding communication barriers |
| | Reflecting feelings (role play) |
| | Knowing when to seek adult help |
| | Peer safety action plan |
| | Practicing help seeking and support (role play) |
| | Assertive communication (role play) |
| | Assertive skills for conflict resolution (role play) |
| | Assertive communication when conflict escalates (role play) |
| | Verbal apology (role play) |
| | Respectfully ending a relationship (role play) |
| | Coping when a relationship ends |
| | Delay, negotiation, refusal skills (role play) |
| | Skills/strategies to build healthy social and intimate relationships (graffiti) |
| | Support |

# References

Catalano, R. F., Berglund, M. L., Ryan, J. A. M., Lonczak, H. S., & Hawkins, J. D. (2004). Positive youth development in the United States: Research findings on evaluations of positive youth development programs. *Annals of the American Academy of Political and Social Science, 591,* 98–124.

Collaborative for Academic, Social, and Emotional Learning. (2013). *Implementing systemic district and school social and emotional learning.* Chicago, IL: Author.

Crooks, C. V., Chiodo, D., Dunlop, C., Lapointe, A., & Kerry, A. (2018). The Fourth R: Considerations for implementing evidence-based healthy relationships and mental health promotion programming in diverse contexts. In A. W. Leschied, D. Saklofske, & G. Flett (Eds.), *The handbook of implementation of school based mental programs.* New York, NY: Springer Publishing.

Crooks, C. V., Scott, K. L., Ellis, W., & Wolfe, D. A. (2011). Impact of a universal school-based violence prevention program on violent delinquency: Distinctive benefits for youth with maltreatment histories. *Child Abuse & Neglect, 35*, 393–400.

Crooks, C. V., Scott, K. L., Wolfe, D. A., Chiodo, D., & Killip, S. (2007). Understanding the link between childhood maltreatment and violent delinquency: What do schools have to add? *Child Maltreatment, 12*, 269–280.

Crooks, C. V., Zwicker, J., Wells, L., Hughes, R., Langlois, A., & Emery, J. C. (2017). Estimating costs and benefits associated with evidence-based violence prevention: Four case studies based on the Fourth R program. *The School of Public Policy, SPP Research Papers, 10*(10), 1–27.

Domitrovich, C. E., Durlak, J. A., Staley, K. C., & Weissberg, R. P. (2017). Social-emotional competence: An essential factor for promoting positive adjustment and reducing risk in school children. *Child Development, 88*(2), 408–416.

Durlak, J. A., Weissberg, R. P., Dymnicki, A. B., Taylor, R. D., & Schellinger, K. B. (2011). The impact of enhancing students' social and emotional learning: A meta-analysis of school-based universal interventions. *Child Development, 82*, 405–432.

Exner-Cortens, D., Wolfe, D., Crooks, C. V., & Chiodo, D. (2019). A preliminary randomized controlled evaluation of a universal healthy relationships promotion program for youth. *Canadian Journal of School Psychology*, 0829573518821508.

Greenberg, M. T., Weissberg, R. P., O'Brien, M. U., Zins, J. E., Fredericks, L., Resnik, H., & Elias, M. J. (2003). Enhancing school-based prevention and youth development through coordinated social, emotional, and academic learning. *American Psychologist, 58*, 466–474.

Lapointe, A., & Crooks, C. V. (2018). *GSA members' experiences with a structured program to promote wellbeing*. Manuscript submitted for publication.

Lapshina, N., Crooks, C. V., & Kerry, A. (2018). *Changes in depression and anxiety among youth in a healthy relationships program: A latent class growth analysis*. Manuscript submitted for publication.

Nation, M., Crusto, C., Wandersman, A., Kumpfer, K. L., Seybolt, D., Morrissey-Kane, E., … Davino, K. (2003). What works in prevention—Principles of effective prevention programs. *American Psychologist, 58*(6–7), 449–456.

Taylor, R. D., Oberle, E., Durlak, J. A., & Weissberg, R. P. (2017). Promoting positive youth development through school-based social and emotional learning interventions: A meta-analysis of follow-up effects. *Child Development, 88*(4), 1156–1171.

Wolfe, D. A., Crooks, C. V., Chiodo, D., Hughes, R., & Ellis, W. (2012). Observations of adolescent peer resistance skills following a classroom-based healthy relationship program: A post-intervention comparison. *Prevention Science, 13*, 196–205.

Wolfe, D. A., Crooks, C. V., Jaffe, P. G., Chiodo, D., Hughes, R., Ellis, W., … Donner, A. (2009). A universal school-based program to prevent adolescent dating violence: A cluster randomized trial. *Archives of Pediatric and Adolescent Medicine, 163*, 693–699.

Wolfe, D. A., Jaffe, P., & Crooks, C. (2006). *Adolescent risk behaviors: Why teens experiment and strategies to keep them safe*. New Haven, CT: Yale University Press.

# Chapter 3
# The Influence of Trauma Exposure on Children's Outcomes

**Brenda Jones Harden, Laura Jimenez Parra, and Aimee Drouin Duncan**

## 3.1 Introduction

All children should experience safety, stability, and stimulation from nurturing caregivers, who could be parents, other relatives, or persons external to the family, such as teachers. Unfortunately, the lives of many children are marked by exposure to traumatic events that potentially derail their development. For example, studies document that approximately 60% of children from newborns to 17 years of age have been exposed to violence in their homes and communities (Finkelhor, Turner, Ormrod, & Hamby, 2009). According to the latest national data (US Department of Health and Human Services, 2017), approximately 676,000 children are victims of child maltreatment annually, at a rate of 9.1 victims per 1000 children.

In this chapter, we review the sequelae of trauma exposure on children's outcomes. We begin by providing a framework for considering trauma's effects on children; we then summarize the research on trauma exposure and children's outcomes across developmental and functional domains. Consistent with this volume's focus, we briefly explore the implications of the impact of trauma exposure for the interventions schools can provide for affected children.

B. J. Harden (✉)

Institute for Child Study, Department of Human Development and Quantitative Methodology, University of Maryland College Park, College Park, MD, USA
e-mail: bjharden@umd.edu

L. J. Parra · A. D. Duncan
University of Maryland College Park, College Park, MD, USA

© Springer Nature Switzerland AG 2019
C. C. Panlilio (ed.), *Trauma-Informed Schools*, Child Maltreatment Solutions
Network, https://doi.org/10.1007/978-3-030-12811-1_3

## 3.2   Definitional and Conceptual Framework

Based on the definition promulgated by the National Child Traumatic Stress Network (NCTSN, 2018), trauma occurs when a child witnesses or experiences an event that poses a real or perceived threat. NCTSN further delineates three types of trauma: acute (i.e., a single event), chronic (i.e., multiple or enduring or recurring events), and/or complex (i.e., multiple traumatic events, often of an invasive, interpersonal nature). A range of events are considered traumatic for children, including:

- Serious illness, such as hospitalization or painful treatments
- Accidents (e.g., car accidents, dog bites, near drownings)
- Separation from caregivers through foster care placement or the death of a parent
- Natural or human-caused disasters like hurricanes, droughts, famine, or war
- Poverty-related factors that compromise safety and security through a lack of resources to fulfill basic needs such as satisfying hunger
- Violent events both internal and external to the family such as intimate partner violence or community violence

Finally, children may be the victims of complex, interpersonal trauma emerging from experiences of sexual and physical abuse, as well as neglect, the most common form of child maltreatment. For the purposes of this paper, our primary focus is interpersonal and complex trauma, specifically child maltreatment.

According to Shonkoff, Boyce, and McEwen (2009), trauma is one of the primary causes of "toxic stress," which they define as the experience of overwhelming environmental stressors that leads to overactivation of the body's stress-response system. The toxic stress emanating from trauma exposure precipitates significant developmental and life course challenges. It can disrupt brain architecture, compromise physiological and psychological responses to future stressors, limit cognitive development, and increase lifelong vulnerability to stress-related illnesses (Shonkoff, 2010). Shonkoff et al. (2009) underscore the pivotal role of caregiving in the experience of stress. Compromised caregiving drives stress to damaging levels, yet supportive caregiving can buffer children against the impact of toxic stress.

## 3.3   Sequelae of Trauma Exposure

Trauma has a pernicious impact on children's outcomes across ages and developmental domains. There is some research that young children are more susceptible to the negative effects of trauma, as they are exposed to trauma at a time of very rapid brain development and behavioral change (Jones Harden, Buhler, & Jimenez Parra, 2016). As the model from NCTSN suggests, trauma's impact on early neurobiology has implications for children's physical, cognitive, language, and socioemotional skills, as well as their physical and mental health. In this section, we briefly summarize the empirical work on the developmental sequelae of trauma exposure from infancy through adolescence.

### 3.3.1 Neurobiological Sequelae

Jaffee and Christian (2014) reviewed the empirical literature on the sequelae of trauma and concluded that trauma is "biologically embedded" in the developing brain. These neurobiological effects lead to a cascade of developmental challenges for affected children across multiple domains that persist over time. In this section, we summarize the current research on the effects of trauma on the brain and other physiological systems.

Infancy and early childhood are characterized by rapid brain growth and development. Particularly marked by the process of synaptogenesis, infants' synapses in the brain increase 500% by the time children are 2 years old. This rapid brain growth is highly dependent on a child's early experiences and external stimuli, making infancy and early childhood sensitive periods of brain development. Young children require appropriate and responsive care and stimulation in order to allow for optimal growth, adaptation, and enhancement of brain circuitry (Sheridan & Nelson, 2009). The normal development of neurobiological pathways can be altered, however, when children (such as those who experience maltreatment) lack appropriate stimuli and enriching experiences during this sensitive period (National Scientific Council on the Developing Child, 2008). Research on the relationship between maltreatment and brain development in early childhood has found significant negative effects on both the structure and function of the brain, which influence hormonal production and have damaging, rippling consequences across different developmental domains (Jaffee & Christian, 2014; National Scientific Council on the Developing Child, 2008; Teicher & Samson, 2016).

The volume and structure of the brain appear to be directly influenced by poor living conditions early in life. Researchers studying young children who were deprived of appropriate and supportive care in institutions have found significant decreases in overall brain size and volume. A decrease was particularly notable in children's prefrontal cortex, often associated with complex cognitive tasks such as decision-making, emotion regulation, and executive function (Perry, 2008; Sheridan & Nelson, 2009). Studies have also found that early adverse experiences are related to decreased volume of the corpus callosum, the fibers that connect both brain hemispheres (Sheridan, Fox, Zeanah, McLaughlin, & Nelson, 2012; Mehta et al., 2009).

Other structural studies in early childhood have focused on the limbic system, specifically the size of the amygdala, typically linked with memory, decision-making, and emotion processing. While it is now widely understood that the amygdala is highly vulnerable to early stress exposure, results of studies looking at the relationship between maltreatment and amygdala volume are inconsistent (Teicher & Samson, 2016). Some research has found smaller amygdala volumes in 9- to

15-year-old children who had experienced physical abuse or neglect in early childhood compared with children of similar socioeconomic background that had not experienced these adverse conditions (Hanson et al., 2015). Other studies, however, focusing on young children living in orphanages, have detailed larger amygdala volumes (Mehta et al., 2009; Tottenham et al., 2010). Researchers have hypothesized that early exposure to trauma and maltreatment may result in an increased size of the amygdala observable in young children, but as a person grows, the severity and timing of maltreatment could sensitize the amygdala to stress and result in the substantial volume reduction typically observed in adolescents and adults (Teicher & Samson, 2016).

Additionally, because of the susceptibility of the limbic system to stress and trauma, extensive research has been conducted on the effects of maltreatment on the functioning of the hypothalamic-pituitary-adrenal (HPA) axis and its production of cortisol. Studies have consistently found that prolonged and chronic exposure to stress alters the function and patterns of the HPA system in young children (Cicchetti, Rogosch, Toth, & Sturge-Apple, 2011). Findings on specific pathways by which the HPA axis and consequent cortisol levels are damaged by these adverse experiences, however, are contradictory. A blunted response (i.e., low cortisol levels) of diurnal cortisol patterns has been reported in multiple studies with infants and young children exposed to stress and trauma early in life (Bernard, Dozier, Bick, & Gordon, 2015; Cicchetti et al., 2011; Dozier et al., 2006). Alternatively, abnormally high cortisol production throughout the day has also been reported in other studies with children experiencing similar adverse conditions (Ivars et al., 2015).

Similar to the conflicting findings in research looking at the structure of the amygdala, discrepancies in the cortisol production of maltreated children may be explained by the type and timing of maltreatment, presence of a psychological disorder, or the time of the day cortisol samples are collected. Physical abuse and physical neglect may be associated with the blunted cortisol diurnal patterns, while emotional abuse and children who experience multiple forms of maltreatment may exhibit higher diurnal cortisol levels (Bruce, Fisher, Pears, & Levine, 2009; Cicchetti & Rogosch, 2001). Nonetheless, it is evident from substantial research that prolonged stress and traumatic experiences such as maltreatment early in life significantly alter normative cortisol production (Cicchetti, Rogosch, Gunnar, & Toth, 2010; Gonzalez, 2013).

Research of the neurobiological sequelae of maltreatment in middle childhood reveals patterns that are similar to research that focuses on young children. Studies have found that the corpus callosum appears to be the brain structure most susceptible to the effect of maltreatment during middle childhood (Andersen et al., 2008). Research on 8- to 11-year-old children who were institutionalized early in childhood and suffered from severe social deprivation showed that they had significantly smaller corpus callosum volumes compared to age-matched children who had not been institutionalized. This difference, however, was only significant for children who had not been assigned to high-quality foster care around 15 months old. While the volume of the corpus callosum was still smaller than age-matched children who had not been institutionalized, a supportive environment early in life appeared to facilitate gains in the size of children's corpus callosum (Sheridan et al., 2012).

Comparable to research conducted with children in early childhood, maltreatment may disrupt the body's cortisol production in middle childhood as well. Altered responses observed in middle childhood, however, may be influenced by the timing of maltreatment and the psychological well-being of the child. A study found that children between 9 and 13 years old who experienced physical and sexual abuse in the first 5 years of life and reported high internalizing symptoms had blunted diurnal cortisol patterns when compared to children who had experienced maltreatment after the age of 5 and children in the aged-matched control group who had not experienced any adverse conditions (Cicchetti et al., 2010). This and similar studies suggest that the disruption of diurnal cortisol patterns emerges and is more prominent when maltreatment occurs in early childhood. However, the altered cortisol production may persist through middle childhood and even into adulthood (Gonzalez, 2013).

There has recently been a surge of research on the role of maltreatment in the regulation of other hormones and neurobiological processes. Researchers have targeted the effect of maltreatment on the body's regulation of oxytocin, typically associated with emotion recognition, attachment, and the stress-response system. While this relationship is just starting to be investigated, studies have found significant disruptions in oxytocin levels in individuals with a history of maltreatment (De Bellis & Zisk, 2014). Seltzer, Ziegler, Connolly, Prososki, and Pollak (2014) found gender differences in maltreated children between 8 and 11 years of age. The study found higher levels of oxytocin in girls with a history of physical abuse compared to girls who had not experienced maltreatment, both at baseline and following a social stress task. In contrast, no significant differences in oxytocin levels were found in the boys who had experienced maltreatment and those who had not faced these adverse experiences. The mechanism and reasoning for these gender differences remains unclear, but the authors theorized high oxytocin levels to be an adaptive response related to hormonal puberty changes (Seltzer et al., 2014). Similar gender differences have been found in research with adults, yet studies with adults have shown blunted oxytocin responses to stress. Women that experienced maltreatment early in childhood, specifically emotional abuse, have been found to have decreased oxytocin levels following a stress task compared to men as a group and women who had not experienced childhood abuse (De Bellis & Zisk, 2014).

Moreover, adverse conditions in early childhood have also been found to affect telomere length, which is partly responsible for cellular aging and associated with multiple health outcomes in adulthood (De Bellis & Zisk, 2014). Research on institutionalized children, for instance, revealed that exposure to extreme social deprivation early in childhood was associated with significantly shorter telomere lengths when they were between 6 and 10 years of age (Drury et al., 2012). Additionally, in a longitudinal study, children who experienced two or more types of violence, such as bullying, domestic violence, and physical abuse, had higher rates of telomere shortening compared to children of similar socioeconomic backgrounds who had not experienced violence (Shalev et al., 2013). Thus, the faster deterioration of telomeres that appears to occur in children who have experienced maltreatment is theorized to contribute to premature aging and subsequent chronic health problems in adulthood (De Bellis & Zisk, 2014).

Literature on maltreatment and its neurobiological consequences during adolescence is scarce, and most studies focus on the effects of early childhood adverse experiences on teens. Some longitudinal studies, however, have found similar detrimental neurobiological patterns as those young maltreated children face. For example, one study examined the effects of maltreatment on the superior longitudinal fasciculus, the pathway responsible for connecting the parietal and frontal cortical regions (i.e., connecting somatosensory information to the prefrontal cortex). Adolescents with a history of physical abuse, sexual abuse, or witnessing domestic violence, for instance, have displayed a reduced integrity of this pathway as well as decreased volume of the corpus callosum (Huang, Gundapuneedi, & Rao, 2012).

A unique neuroimaging study on maltreated adolescents documented larger left hippocampal volumes and decreased growth of the left amygdala over time (Whittle et al., 2013). Additionally, for adolescents experiencing psychopathology, maltreatment was associated with decreased growth of the left hippocampus and increased growth of the left amygdala over time (Whittle et al., 2013). The researchers also found age effects related to adverse experiences in the volume of the participants' amygdala. While maltreatment was not associated with amygdala volume in early adolescence, when participants were 12 years old, maltreatment was significantly related to decreased amygdala growth in late adolescence at 15 years of age. The study consequently provides some evidence to the timing effect of maltreatment on amygdala volume. While research on young children reveals increased amygdala volumes, research on older adolescents suggests that maltreatment appears to stunt normative amygdala growth later in life (Whittle et al., 2013).

Altered cortisol production has also been found in adolescents with a maltreatment history. In a longitudinal study following women from 6 to 30 years of age, participants with a history of sexual abuse exhibited blunted diurnal cortisol levels that emerged in mid- to late adolescence (Trickett, Noll, Susman, Shenk, & Putnam, 2010). Similarly, these attenuated cortisol patterns and altered stress response were also observed in female adolescents who had been referred from Child Protective Services for diverse types of abuse or neglect. Notably, low cortisol levels were more strongly associated with adolescents who reported more behavioral and social problems compared to those who reported high internalizing symptoms and were clinically depressed (MacMillan et al., 2009). These studies, like many others studying the relationship between maltreatment and the neurobiological sequelae, focus on maltreatment that occurs in early childhood. Much less is known about the biological consequences of maltreatment that occurs after 5 years of age (De Bellis & Zisk, 2014).

### 3.3.2 Physical Health and Motor Sequelae

Maltreatment in early childhood has particularly detrimental consequences for an infant's physical health and motor functioning. The physical effects of maltreatment can range from immediate to long-term health consequences. Physical abuse can lead to severe injuries such as bruises, broken bones, head trauma, and/or death (U.S. Department of Health and Human Services, 2005). Additionally, physical neglect early in life can lead to significant motor and growth delays in young children (Norman et al., 2012). Research has found that young children who have experienced maltreatment, particularly physical or sexual abuse, show rates of severe motor impairments that are five to seven times higher than those expected from pediatric norms (Wade, Bowden, & Sites, 2018). There is substantial evidence that young children who have faced maltreatment experience higher rates of physical injuries compared to older and non-maltreated children of similar socioeconomic backgrounds. Research has found that these injuries tend to occur because of parents' lack of knowledge regarding children's developmental capacities, environmental hazards, and lack of child supervision (Dubowitz & Black, 2002; Jones Harden et al., 2016).

Abusive head trauma, commonly referred to as "shaken baby syndrome," is particularly prevalent in children under the age of 2 and leads to a host of negative outcomes. Short-term consequences of this abuse include, but are not limited to, hearing loss, blindness, retinal hemorrhaging, impaired motor control, and seizures. Mortality rates for infants who have experienced abusive head trauma are very high (11–36%) due to infants' vulnerability to head injuries. Moreover, abusive head trauma has been found to be associated with developmental, social, cognitive, and language delays (Chevignard & Lind, 2014; Christian & Block, 2009).

Exposure to maltreatment early in childhood can also lead to a compromised immune system, leading to chronic inflammation, multiple adverse health outcomes, and heightened immune response to stressors (Slopen, Kubzansky, McLaughlin, & Koenen, 2013). The immune system plays a crucial role in the body's response to pathogens and stressors, activating inflammatory responses and markers such as C-reactive protein, associated with the body's regulation and defense against infection. The disruption of these normative inflammatory responses as a result of childhood maltreatment has been consistently linked with chronic diseases in childhood and cardiovascular and autoimmune problems in adulthood (Gonzalez, 2013). Using the National Survey of Child and Adolescent Well-Being II, Kerker et al. (2015) found a significant relation between the Adverse Childhood Experiences (ACEs) score and chronic diseases in children ages 2–6. With every additional reported ACE score from the average of 3.6, there was a 21% increased chance of suffering from a chronic medical condition (Kerker et al., 2015). Research has also found that children who have experienced physical abuse or neglect have a significantly lower pediatric health-related quality of life compared to age-matched children of similar socioeconomic status. Children who have experienced these types of adverse experiences have lower total, physical, and psychosocial health (Lanier, Kohl, Raghavan, & Auslander, 2015).

Research on the effects of maltreatment on the physical health and motor functioning of children in middle childhood is limited. Studies have primarily focused on the health outcomes of young children and adults when chronic diseases are more prevalent. Several studies on adults have found, for example, multiple irregularities in the brain and the endocrine and immune systems associated with childhood maltreatment and current depression. Adults who experienced maltreatment in their childhood have higher rates of inflammation, arthritis, cardiovascular disease, cancer, and overall reduced life expectancy. Additionally, evidence suggests that adverse experiences in childhood are significantly associated with higher rates of risky behaviors in adulthood, leading to higher rates of smoking, drug use, and sexually transmitted infections (Norman et al., 2012). Consistent with adult studies, researchers examining the relationship between maltreatment and the immune system response found elevated levels of C-reactive protein (CRP) in 12-year-old physically abused children who also suffered from depression. Notably, high levels of CRP were only found in children who were maltreated during the first decade of life and presented high depression symptoms, compared with children who only presented depression symptoms, those who were only maltreated in childhood, and control children. These elevated inflammation responses were significantly related to maltreatment, regardless of the children's socioeconomic status, gender, and body temperature (Danese et al., 2011).

Further, the detrimental effects of maltreatment on motor development have rarely been studied during the middle childhood period. One of the first studies to address this relationship found that 8- to 9-year-old children who suffered from parental neglect and witnessed domestic violence presented a variety of motor delays. Specifically, researchers found that the high-risk environments of maltreated children were significantly associated with children's balance abilities compared to children who had not experienced adverse childhood conditions. Maltreatment, however, did not appear to negatively affect children's manual dexterity or their performance on aiming and catching tasks. Physical neglect and less apparent forms of adverse experiences such as witnessing domestic violence seem to influence motor functioning in more subtle ways as well. Nevertheless, more research is needed to understand the relationship between maltreatment and motor functioning during middle childhood (Sartori, Bandeira, Nobre, da Silva Ramalho, & Valentini, 2017).

The detrimental health effects of maltreatment in adolescence reveal similar patterns to the health outcomes in adults. Most of the literature examining this relation has focused on the effects of sexual abuse on adolescents' health outcomes. Childhood sexual abuse has been significantly associated with sleep problems in adolescent girls, even after controlling for psychological disorders often related to sleep disorders such as depression and PTSD (Noll, Haralson, Butler, & Shenk, 2011). Additionally, sexual abuse has been primarily associated with earlier onset of puberty in females. Research found that the rates of puberty onset occurred in females with a history of sexual abuse around 8–12 months earlier compared to control participants matched in terms of socioeconomic status, age, and ethnicity. This earlier onset of puberty may, then, increase the occurrence of risky behaviors and psychological disorders in adolescence (Noll et al., 2017; Trickett, Negriff, Ji, & Peckins, 2011).

Evidence that maltreatment increases the frequency of risky behaviors has been mostly studied through adolescents' substance use. While substance use increases substantially in mid- to late adolescence, extensive research has found that maltreatment is linked with higher rates of substance use. In a sample of 12- to 17-year-old adolescents ($n = 281$) who met criteria for substance abuse, around 60% of the participants reported some form of childhood maltreatment. Adolescents with a history of physical and sexual abuse seem to be particularly at risk for substance abuse or dependence on alcohol, marijuana, and other hard drugs (Trickett et al., 2011). Despite these significant findings, further research needs to be conducted to examine the relationship between maltreatment and children's physical health and motor functioning during middle childhood and adolescence to understand the development of chronic health issues that are observed later in adulthood (Pollak, 2015).

### 3.3.3 Cognitive-Academic Sequelae

The detrimental cognitive and academic sequelae of early childhood maltreatment have been well documented. Exposure to adverse experiences early in childhood is consistently associated with critical lags in cognitive development and numerous academic difficulties (De Bellis, Hooper, Spratt, & Woolley, 2009; Gould et al., 2012). Cross-sectional studies have documented high rates of cognitive developmental delays (13–62%) in infants and toddlers placed in foster care due to abuse or neglect (Leslie, Gordon, Ganger, & Gist, 2002). Findings from the National Survey of Child and Adolescent Well-Being (NSCAW), a nationally representative sample of children in the welfare system, reveal that more than half of maltreated children under the age of 2 appear to be at risk for developmental delays (Dolan et al., 2011). Children in this sample who experienced physical abuse and neglect scored lower on cognitive development tests compared to non-maltreated children (Jones Harden & Whittaker, 2011). Earlier studies have also revealed that maltreated children under the age of 3 are at higher risk for an array of cognitive difficulties, specifically poor problem-solving skills, lower IQs, and reduced language abilities (Cicchetti & Carlson, 1989; Erickson, Egeland, & Pianta, 1989).

The relationship between child maltreatment and cognitive development has been particularly evident in research involving institutionalized Romanian children whose infancy was characterized with severe physical and emotional neglect. Several studies have found significant deficits in these children's intellectual functioning, attention, language skills, and memory when compared to aged-matched children who had not experienced these neglectful adverse conditions (Chugani et al., 2001; Mills et al., 2010; Nelson et al., 2007). Studies have also focused on the effect of maltreatment on children's executive functioning abilities. Executive function comprises skills related to children's cognitive inhibition and flexibility, attention, and working memory. Research has found that maltreatment has negative repercussions for young children's executive functioning skills. Physical and emotional neglect has been associated with deficiencies in children's abilities to retain and manipulate information, as evidenced by maltreated children's performance in spatial working memory and facial memory tasks (Pollak et al., 2010) and less flexibility and creativity in problem-solving tasks (Levendosky, Okun, & Parker, 1995), as well as overall poor school readiness and compromised attention, reasoning, and executive function (Bos, Fox, Zeanah, & Nelson, 2009; Brassard & Gelardo, 1987; De Bellis et al., 2002).

Studies conducted with maltreated children have also revealed that these cognitive difficulties could be particularly influenced by the type of maltreatment the child has suffered. In a longitudinal study investigating the links between early maltreatment and consequent preschool outcomes, Egeland, Sroufe, and Erickson (1983) found specific forms of cognitive delays based on the type of early childhood maltreatment. Children who had been physically abused presented less focus and persistence in tasks compared to the other preschoolers who had experienced different types of maltreatment. In contrast, neglect was significantly associated with poor impulse control and less use of creativity in problem-solving tasks. Additionally, out of all the children in the sample, those who had been physically neglected had the lowest scores on the intellectual functioning standardized tests administered (Egeland et al.). More recently, a study of 12- to 47-month-old children revealed differences in the cognitive outcomes of children depending on the type of maltreatment. Physical abuse and neglect were significantly associated with delayed growth in language abilities, while sexual abuse appeared to significantly hinder children's cognitive development (Stahmer et al., 2009).

These early childhood cognitive impairments have significant implications for later academic success. For example, the impact of neglect in early childhood appears to be most strongly associated with poor academic achievement. A study of 4- to 6-year-old children from low socioeconomic backgrounds revealed that children who had experienced neglect early in life had significantly lower scores on both kindergarten and first grade assessments when compared to children from similar backgrounds who had not experienced neglect (Manly, Lynch, Oshri, Herzog, & Wortel, 2013).

Studies examining the consequences of maltreatment on school-aged children's cognitive development have focused primarily on children with adverse experiences in early childhood, before the child is 5 years old. Limited research has examined the sequelae of maltreatment that occurs during middle childhood. Earlier studies suggested that maltreatment is associated with poor academic performance (Kelley, Thornberry, & Smith, 1997; Kurtz, Gaudin Jr., Wodarski, & Howing, 1993; Wodarski, Kurtz, Gaudin Jr., & Howing, 1990). More recently, children between 10 and 12 years of age who had experienced emotional abuse or physical neglect earlier in life presented lower intelligence scores and poorer decision-making skills compared to children from the same socioeconomic background. Moreover, physical abuse was significantly related to deficiencies in problem-solving skills (Fishbein et al., 2009). Neglect has also been found to have particularly detrimental effects on children's numeracy and literacy skills, with several studies linking grade repetition to a child's neglectful environment (Maguire et al., 2015).

Longitudinal research using data from the Fragile Families and Child Well-Being Study has found that while the detrimental cognitive effects of maltreatment occur rapidly and early in life, they may be further exacerbated by newly occurring adverse experiences and trauma over time (Font & Berger, 2015). Early childhood physical neglect was strongly associated with reduced receptive and expressive vocabulary skills at age 3, and these reduced abilities were moderately associated with children's poor cognitive skills between 3 and 9 years of age. Additionally, maltreatment in infancy and toddlerhood appear to have a more significant effect on children's cognitive development compared to maltreatment that occurs after the child is 3 years old. Findings revealed a stronger association between early occurrence of physical neglect (1–3 years old) with adverse cognitive outcomes later in a child's life (both 5 and 9 years old) compared to the cognitive deficits seen when maltreatment occurred between 3 and 5 years of age (Font & Berger, 2015).

The negative cognitive and academic effects of maltreatment in early childhood appear to follow children well into adolescence. A large longitudinal study composed of 7223 participants examined the association between childhood abuse and neglect and long-term cognitive outcomes. While there were substantial attrition rates in the study, particularly in the group of participants who had been reported to the state as victims of maltreatment, 3796 14-year-old adolescents completed a series of achievement tests and Raven's Standard Progressive Matrices as a measure of cognitive development. The study's findings revealed that abuse and neglect were related to lower scores on both assessments, and both types of maltreatment were independently associated with poor reading skills and lower perceptual reasoning scores. Further, while different types of maltreatment typically co-occurred, abuse and neglect early in childhood were both independently associated with deficits in cognition and academic achievement in adolescence (Mills et al., 2010).

Additionally, multiple studies examining the effects of early childhood maltreatment in adolescence report impaired academic achievement, as evidenced by higher rates of grade retention, lower overall grades, and greater special education needs in maltreated adolescents. Maltreated adolescents are also at greater risk for not completing high school (Lemkin, Kistin, Cabral, Aschengrau, & Bair-Merritt, 2018). These academic sequelae of maltreatment in adolescence may be partially explained by the cascading cognitive, social, and neurobiological consequences that abuse and neglect have on children beginning earlier in life. The disruption of these key developmental processes early in childhood, combined with the damaging environmental characteristics to which maltreated children are typically exposed, may lead to the numerous academic difficulties of maltreated adolescents (Romano, Babchishin, Marquis, & Fréchette, 2015).

### 3.3.4 Language Sequelae

Language is a core developmental process that is related to a host of other outcomes in children, including academic achievement, prosocial skills, and behavior problems (Gleason & Ratner, 2009). Despite the extensive knowledge about the development of language and its importance for outcomes across childhood (e.g., Tamis-LeMonda & Rodriguez, 2009), few studies have been conducted that examine the link between child maltreatment and language skills. The available literature does suggest that maltreated children may not have the positive caregiving experiences that promote these capacities and thus are at risk for language delays (Aber & Cicchetti, 1984; Shirk, 1988; Spratt et al., 2012). The linguistic experiences of these children are often characterized by more simplistic language, fewer questions, and less positive and empathetic responses (Christopolous, Bonvillian, & Crittenden, 1988; Eigsti & Cicchetti, 2004). Jones Harden and Whittaker (2011) documented that maltreated preschool children who lived with greater numbers of children and whose homes were less cognitively stimulating and emotionally supportive incurred more compromised language outcomes.

Because early childhood is the sensitive period for language development (Gleason & Ratner, 2009; Tamis-LeMonda & Rodriguez, 2009), young maltreated children are at particular risk for language delays. In a meta-analytic review of studies examining maltreatment and language, it was documented that the language skills of children who have experienced abuse or neglect are delayed when compared to children without such experience, with young children being particularly vulnerable to the language effects of maltreatment (Sylvestre, Bussières, & Bouchard, 2016). In a study of young children in the child welfare system, language delays were estimated at rates of one in four (26.0%) in children under 6 (Casanueva et al., 2012). This study documented an association between maltreatment and diminished receptive language, the ability to understand language, and expressive language, the ability to articulate language (Casanueva et al., 2012). Maltreated children's expressive language seems to be particularly compromised (Casanueva et al., 2012; Fox, Long, & Langlois, 1988), with delays found to persist over time (Jacobsen, Moe, Ivarsson, Wentzel-Larsen, & Smith, 2013).

Maltreatment status in children has been connected to fewer mean length utterances (i.e., units of sounds) and use of fewer abstract words (Coster, Gersten, Beeghly, & Cicchetti, 1989). Maltreated children use fewer words in general, compose less complex sentence structures, and have more difficulty articulating ideas with confidence (Coster & Cicchetti, 1993; Eigsti & Cicchetti, 2004; Gersten, Coster, Schneider-Rosen, Carlson, & Cicchetti, 1986). They also use less self-referential speech, such as fewer first person pronouns and mentions of their own internal states and behaviors, and articulate more negative self-perceptions (Herrenkohl, Herrenkohl, Toedter, & Yanushefski, 1984; McFadyen & Kitson, 1996).

The literature is very sparse with respect to maltreatment effects on language development beyond the early childhood period. Wodarski and colleagues (1990) documented that neglected—but not abused—school-aged children had lower scores than comparison children on a standardized basic language skills test. Similarly, O'Hara and colleagues (2015) found that young school-aged children who were only victims of neglect displayed more compromised vocabularies than children who were both neglected and abused. In a unique study of adolescents, McFadyen and Kitson (1996) documented more compromised syntactic expression, increased self-repetition, and less self-related language among abused adolescents when compared with a non-abused comparison group. However, no differences were found between the comprehension abilities or expressive language skills of the two groups.

Finally, Manso and colleagues conducted a series of within-group studies exploring the language skills of maltreated school-aged children and adolescents in residential foster care. They documented that these children tend to have greater difficulties in pragmatics (i.e., the function of language and how language is used to convey meaning in a specific context) and morphology (the structure and parts of words) than in the syntax (i.e., grammar; structure of sentences) and semantics (meanings of signs, symbols, and words) of language (Manso, 2009; Manso, García-Baamonde, Alonso, & Barona, 2010; Manso, Sánchez, & Alonso, 2012).

There is some evidence that distinct forms of maltreatment differentially impact language development. Neglected children show worse language comprehension, as well as more compromised receptive and expressive language (Culp et al., 1991; Fox et al., 1988; Gersten et al., 1986; Pears & Fisher, 2005; Spratt et al., 2012) than non-maltreated or abused children. Studies of children in foster care confirm that those referred for neglect have more negative language outcomes than children referred for both abuse and neglect (Allen & Oliver, 1982). Further, in a within-group study of neglected children, language delay was associated with maternal physical and emotional abuse experience as a child and the mother's low acceptability level toward her child (Sylvestre & Mérette, 2010). Children identified as victims of neglect may have experienced sustained experiences of language deprivation through the lack of interaction with their caregivers (Culp et al., 1991).

Language delays among maltreated children can have a deleterious effect on other developmental arenas. Language competency is a strong indicator of children's school readiness with respect to literacy, compliance with teachers, performance evaluation, and peer interactions (Coster & Cicchetti, 1993; Stock & Fisher, 2006). Further, when children lack age-level language capacities, later behavior and mental health problems may arise (Spratt et al., 2012).

## 3.3.5 Social-Emotional Sequelae

Social-emotional development entails the capacity to understand the self and others, to form relationships, and to experience, regulate, and express emotions. Children's social-emotional competence depends on the quality of relationships and the environment that they experience and is detrimentally affected by the experience of trauma and stress (Thompson, 2016). Trauma, compounded by family poverty or other environmental stressors, can impact children's social-emotional development through impaired attachment (Egeland & Sroufe, 1981). When the attachment relationship is compromised by trauma or maltreatment, including nonresponsive or unpredictable caregiving, insecure attachment patterns can result (Bos et al., 2009; Mickelson, Kessler, & Shaver, 1997). It is difficult for maltreated children to be securely attached because their caregivers, instead of being the source of comfort and reassurance, are the cause of fear and harm (Hesse & Main, 2006).

Multiple studies have documented that maltreated children display insecure attachment, particularly disorganized attachment, to their caregivers (Cassidy & Shaver, 2002; Lyons-Ruth & Block, 1996; Scheeringa, Zeanah, Myers, & Putnam, 2003). A meta-analysis of the association between child maltreatment and disorganized attachment revealed that maltreated children are more likely to display disorganized attachment and less likely to present secure attachment when compared to non-maltreated high-risk children (Cyr, Euser, Bakermans-Kranenburg, & Van Ijzendoorn, 2010). Insecure attachment patterns and sustained childhood trauma disrupt self-regulatory abilities and may lead to compromised affect, consciousness, behavior, cognition, and sense of self (Cook et al., 2017). In particular, disorganized attachment in children has been linked to behavior problems and dissociative symptoms (Bernard et al., 2015; Cyr et al., 2010).

Additionally, studies have shown that maltreatment influences emotion expression and understanding. In one study, maltreated children exhibited more anger and less positive affect compared to non-maltreated children (Robinson et al., 2009). Shaffer, Huston, and Egeland (2008) found that sexually maltreated girls displayed less capacity for emotion understanding than their non-maltreated peers. Further, these girls expected less emotional support and more relational conflict from parents in response to sadness displays and from parents and peers in response to anger displays. In another study, maltreated children displayed faster reaction times than children in control groups when labeling emotional facial expressions, particularly fearful faces (Masten et al., 2008). Similarly, in a study of adolescents, maltreatment was related to better recognition of fear and sadness (Leist & Dadds, 2009).

Findings from studies conducted by Pollak and colleagues (e.g., Goldsmith, Pollak, & Davidson, 2008; Romens & Pollak, 2012) suggest that maltreated children may exhibit emotion understanding capacities that are different from their non-maltreated counterparts. For example, abused children may be more attuned to the expression of negative emotions, such as anger, and neglected children may be less able to discern distinctions between emotions. However, in a small study of young children in foster care, language was the most important predictor of emotion understanding, rather than factors such as maltreatment type and the stability of foster care placement (Jones Harden, Morrison, & Clyman, 2014). In another study, severely maltreated children were observed to avoid attending to threatening faces (Pine et al., 2005), which was conceptualized as children's attention bias away from threat.

Maltreatment also affects children's emotion regulation, which is defined as a biologically based and environmentally mediated process through which children adapt and cope with their emotions when responding to stimuli (Cole, Martin, & Dennis, 2004; Thompson, 1994). Exposure to maltreating parents' harsh, inconsistent parenting and negative, dysregulated affect does not facilitate young children's emotion regulation (Kim-Spoon, Cicchetti, & Rogosch, 2013; Maughan & Cicchetti, 2002; Robinson et al., 2009). Many studies have suggested that emotion regulation is the mechanism by which maltreatment leads to psychopathology (Jennissen, Holl, Mai, Wolff, & Barnow, 2016).

For example, in a study of sexually maltreated girls, parental positive affect was associated with lower child internalizing symptomatology, while parental anger was associated with higher child internalizing symptomatology in the entire sample (Shaffer et al., 2008). Another study, which examined 1- to 3-year-olds, found that maltreated children displayed lower positive affect and more anger toward their mothers, which in turn was associated with more internalizing symptoms (Robinson et al., 2009). Finally, a longitudinal study linked emotion dysregulation to multiple maltreatment types and the early onset of maltreatment (Kim & Cicchetti, 2010). Lower emotion regulation was associated with higher externalizing symptomatology, as well as later peer rejection, which in turn was related to higher externalizing symptoms. Conversely, higher emotion regulation was predictive of higher peer acceptance over time, which was related to lower internalizing symptomatology.

Children with a history of traumatic experience and impaired affect regulation may display maladaptive coping strategies (Courtois, 2008; Ford, 2017; Van der Kolk, 2017), thus leading to poor behavior regulation. Maltreated children may be more likely to respond to neutral or negative affect, having not experienced secure attachments (Schneider-Rosen & Cicchetti, 1984; Van der Kolk, Roth, Pelcovitz, Sunday, & Spinazzola, 2005). They may display elevated, negative responses to even minor stressors. Additionally, abused children may demonstrate compulsive compliant behaviors, resistance to change, rigid behavior patterns, aggression, and oppositional behavior (Crittenden & DiLalla, 1988; Ford et al., 2000; Koenig, Cicchetti, & Rogosch, 2000).

Trauma has been associated with a range of social-emotional challenges in young children (Shonkoff & Garner, 2011), which affects their capacity to interact with peers and adults throughout childhood and adolescence. For example, in order to be successful in school, children must relate to teachers and peers in positive ways, regulate emotions to work independently and cooperatively, and attend to instructional cues. Children with compromised socio-emotional development resulting from trauma may exhibit hyperactive behaviors (De Young, Kenardy, & Cobham, 2011), be avoidant or socially withdrawn from social activities or peers (De Young et al., 2011), or display negative affect (Jones & Cureton, 2014). They may also display compromised concentration, hypervigilant or exaggerated responses, anxiety, and aggression (Scheeringa et al., 2003). These conditions and behaviors place the child at risk for a range of social-emotional and mental health difficulties (Thompson, 2016).

### 3.3.6 Mental Health Sequelae

There is substantial evidence that trauma and maltreatment impact children's and adolescents' mental health outcomes. Infants, toddlers, and children who have experienced trauma may experience anxiety, fear, depression, or problems with behavior and impulse control (Scheeringa et al., 2003). Trauma exposure places older children and adolescents at greater risk for psychiatric disorders and symptomatology (Finkelhor, Ormrod, & Turner, 2007; McCart et al., 2007), such as depression, attention-deficit/hyperactivity disorder (ADHD), oppositional defiant disorder (ODD), conduct disorder, anxiety disorders, eating disorders, sleep disorders, communication disorders, separation anxiety disorder, and reactive attachment disorder. Jaffee, Caspi, Moffitt, and Taylor (2004) analyzed a large-scale data set and found that physical maltreatment is related to the development of children's antisocial behavior and that preventing maltreatment can prevent its violent sequelae. In a large-scale study of children in the child welfare system, Casanueva et al. (2012) documented that approximately one fifth of children and adolescents had externalizing or internalizing problems in the clinical range.

Maltreated children may also display symptoms of post-traumatic stress, such as re-experiencing the traumatic event (often through play); avoidance of triggers that remind them of the traumatic experience; hyperarousal; disturbed sleep; increased irritability, aggression, and alertness; temper tantrums; and startled and extreme responses to stimuli (De Young et al., 2011; Scheeringa, Myers, Putnam, & Zeanah, 2015). In a study with 1- to 5-year-old Israeli children (Feldman & Vengrober, 2011), nearly a third of the children suffered from PTSD as a result of being exposed to war. This study also demonstrated that preschoolers (3- to 5-year-olds) were twice as likely as toddlers to develop PTSD.

Researchers have documented that maltreated individuals, who present with depressive, anxiety, and substance use disorders, often have distinct characteristics from non-maltreated individuals with the same diagnoses. They are younger at the onset of the disorder, have more severe symptoms, are more likely to have comorbid disorders, and have a greater risk for suicide and a poorer response to treatment (Teicher & Samson, 2016). Imaging studies conducted on individuals with these disorders demonstrate that they have particular brain characteristics, such as reduced hippocampal volume and amygdala hyper-reactivity (Teicher & Samson, 2013). These brain effects are more consistently observed in maltreated individuals and may represent a maltreatment-related risk factor.

Multiple studies have examined the mechanisms by which maltreatment leads to psychopathology in children. One hypothesis is that maltreated children's compromised emotion regulation leads to a range of mental health difficulties. For example, Alink, Cicchetti, Kim, and Rogosch (2009) examined the roles of emotion regulation and the mother-child relationship quality in psychopathology in maltreated children and found that only emotion regulation affected the relation between maltreatment and psychopathology. For the group of children with an insecure pattern of relatedness, maltreatment was related to lower levels of emotion regulation and, subsequently, higher levels of internalizing and externalizing symptoms.

Further, Egeland, Yates, Appleyard, and Van Dulmen (2002) found that the lack of a close emotional relationship between the child and primary caregiver (alienation) and, to a much lesser extent, dysregulation helped to explain the relation between early maltreatment and later antisocial behavior. Their findings indicated that physical abuse in early childhood, not emotional neglect, led to alienation in preschool, which then predicted externalizing problems in the elementary school years, ultimately resulting in antisocial behavior in adolescence. Such a longitudinal, "developmental cascade" approach was also undertaken in a study by Rogosch, Oshri, and Cicchetti (2010). The authors found an association between child maltreatment and early externalizing and internalizing problems and social competence, as well as to cannabis abuse and dependence (CAD) symptoms in adolescence. Youth CAD symptoms were directly related to child maltreatment and externalizing problems. Childhood internalizing symptoms affected later childhood decrease in social competence, which led to increases in late adolescent externalizing problems.

The association between the overall number of trauma exposures and the severity of psychiatric symptoms tells us little about which forms of trauma may be most detrimental to mental health (Finkelhor et al., 2007). While community and domestic violence are associated with a range of psychiatric symptomatology among youth (Evans, Davies, & DiLillo, 2008; Fowler, Tompsett, Braciszewski, Jacques-Tiura, & Baltes, 2009), fewer comparative studies have explored their specific contributions to mental health outcomes. Overall, research has consistently indicated that trauma may result in impaired capacities for self-regulation and interpersonal relationships. These impaired capacities place children at risk for psychiatric and addictive disorders and chronic medical illness, as well as legal, vocational, and family problems across the lifespan (Allen, Hauser, & Borman-Spurrell, 1996; Mickelson et al., 1997; Waldinger, Schulz, Barsky, & Ahern, 2006).

## 3.4 Summary and Implications for Schools

Based on the review of the previous section, trauma, specifically maltreatment, affects children's outcomes across ages and all domains of health and functioning. Trauma leads to early neurobiological changes that have a cascading impact on children's physical and mental health, cognitive and language skills, and social-emotional functioning. Specifically, maltreatment adversely affects brain regions that are implicated in higher-order thinking as well as emotion and behavioral regulation. This may lead to physiological and physical health impairments that begin in infancy and potentially extend to adulthood, including growth delays, compromised immune systems, altered HPA/stress-response system function, and the sequelae of head trauma. Further, maltreated children and adolescents have high rates of cognitive and language delays; display compromised executive functioning, memory, and problem-solving skills; and, as a result, experience significant academic challenges. Regarding social-emotional functioning, maltreated children and adolescents may have experienced insecure attachment to their caregivers; have impairments in their emotion understanding, expression, and regulation; display symptoms of post-traumatic stress; and have a host of mental health challenges, including internalizing and externalizing disorders.

Thus, it is critical that children who are at risk for or who have been exposed to trauma experience interventions that can potentially attenuate their adverse outcomes. The US Department of Justice's Defending Childhood Initiative (2012) identifies three potential pathways through which trauma can be addressed: (1) directly reducing interpersonal violence, (2) decreasing the environmental risks (e.g., poverty) that place families at risk for experiencing trauma, and (3) developing and increasing the availability of interventions that can buffer young children against the consequences of trauma.

Building on this framework, NCTSN and others have argued for trauma-informed systems in various child-serving contexts. Because the educational system is arguably the largest child-serving system in the USA, schools represent an important context for incorporating trauma-informed approaches. However, schools have not generally capitalized on available resources to create a trauma-informed educational system (Ko et al., 2008). Using multidisciplinary teams of educators, counselors, and other support personnel, a trauma-informed educational system should instill, into their organizational cultures, policies, and practices, knowledge about the impact of traumatic stress on children, parents, caregivers, and service providers (Ko et al., 2008; U.S. Department of Health and Human Services, 2012a). Thus, schools should aim to (1) maximize physical and psychological safety for children and families; (2) identify the trauma-related needs of children and families; (3) enhance the well-being and resilience of children, families, and providers; and (4) partner with children, families, agencies, and systems that interact with children and families (Ko et al., 2008; NCTSN, 2018). As such, a trauma-informed system should incorporate the following strategies:

- Routine screening for trauma exposure and related symptoms
- Culturally appropriate, evidence-based screening, assessment, and treatment for traumatic stress and associated mental health symptoms
- Available resources on trauma exposure, its impact, and treatments
- Efforts to strengthen the resilience and protective factors of children and families affected by and at risk for trauma exposure
- Interventions to address parent and caregiver trauma and its impact on the family system
- Continuity of care and collaboration across child service systems
- An environment of care for staff that addresses, minimizes, and treats secondary traumatic stress and that increases staff resilience.

Because school-based personnel represent proportionally the largest group of professionals referring maltreated children to Child Protective Services (US Department of Health and Human Services, 2017), it is essential that they receive ongoing professional development regarding their roles as mandated reporters and how to make appropriate referrals. Beyond the maltreatment surveillance conducted in school contexts, it is essential that children at risk for trauma experience high-quality schools. Specifically, schools should be physically and psychologically safe havens for children, where they experience stability, nurturance, and appropriate stimulation, predictable daily routines in the school, and nonpunitive discipline (Ko et al., 2008). Additionally, due to their cognitive, language, and academic delays, these children would benefit from interventions to enhance language, learning, and academic skills (Abbott-Shim, Lambert, & McCarty, 2003; Clements, Reynolds, & Hickey, 2004; Love et al., 2005; Ludwig & Phillips, 2008; U.S. Department of Health and Human Services, 2012b).

Additionally, schools can develop and implement interventions to address trauma, many of which emanate from the field of public health. Capitalizing on a public health approach, the National Research Council and Institute of Medicine (2009) argues for a three-tiered approach to the prevention of mental, emotional, and behavioral disorders in children that can inform maltreatment prevention and intervention services. Primary, or universal, prevention programs target entire populations or vulnerable subgroups of a population (e.g., impoverished families) with a goal of preventing a problem's onset. In this vein, schools can provide system- or building-wide trauma-related supports for children that include developmentally appropriate curricula for children, parent education, and professional development for school personnel. Another primary prevention strategy entails using schools as a hub for tangible resources that families need, such as child care resources and food and clothing pantries.

Secondary, or selective, prevention strategies are designed to benefit individuals who display risk for the development of a particular problem. In the school context, counselors and teachers can target interventions for children who present with risk factors for trauma exposure (e.g., extreme and chronic poverty, parental mental illness, familial substance involvement). These interventions may range from providing psychoeducational groups for children to express their concerns about themselves and their families to providing supports for families like establishing parent coffee hours to decrease isolation and receive peer support around parenting and connecting families to community-based resources such as home visiting programs.

Finally, tertiary, or indicated, prevention programs have a goal of preventing the recurrence of a problem and adverse outcomes that emanate from the experience of a particular phenomenon. Tertiary programs target individuals who have already experienced a particular problem and address challenges and sequelae at the individual level. Thus, school-based mental health teams could provide short-term, evidence-based interventions to trauma-affected students and their families that center on understanding trauma and addressing its impact on children and adults alike such as Head Start Trauma Smart (Holmes, Levy, Smith, Pinne, & Neese, 2015) or Cognitive Behavioral Intervention for Trauma in Schools (Stein et al., 2003). In addition to school-based services, these families should be referred to community-based resources for mental health intervention, substance abuse treatment, and child welfare services.

In sum, trauma has deleterious effects on children's physical and mental health, as well as their cognitive, language, and social-emotional development. Schools represent an important context in which to identify children's exposure to trauma and to provide a system of care that can attenuate the impact of trauma exposure. School-based interventions, which should be developmentally informed, can contribute to the promotion of more positive outcomes among this vulnerable group of children. Thus, as the largest child-serving system in the USA, the educational system should embrace a trauma-informed approach to meeting the academic as well as the mental health needs of trauma-exposed children.

# References

Abbott-Shim, M., Lambert, R., & McCarty, F. (2003). A comparison of school readiness outcomes for children randomly assigned to a Head Start program and the program's waitlist. *Journal of Education for Students Placed at Risk (JESPAR), 8*, 191–214.

Aber, J. L., & Cicchetti, D. (1984). The socio-emotional development of maltreated children. In H. Fitzgerald, B. Lester, & M. Yogman (Eds.), *Theory and research in behavioral pediatrics* (pp. 147–205). New York, NY: Springer.

Alink, L. R., Cicchetti, D., Kim, J., & Rogosch, F. A. (2009). Mediating and moderating processes in the relation between maltreatment and psychopathology: Mother-child relationship quality and emotion regulation. *Journal of Abnormal Child Psychology, 37*, 831–843.

Allen, J. P., Hauser, S. T., & Borman-Spurrell, E. (1996). Attachment theory as a framework for understanding sequelae of severe adolescent psychopathology: An 11-year follow-up study. *Journal of Consulting and Clinical Psychology, 64*, 254–263.

Allen, R. E., & Oliver, J. M. (1982). The effects of child maltreatment on language development. *Child Abuse & Neglect, 6*, 299–305.

Andersen, S. L., Tomada, A., Vincow, E. S., Valente, E., Polcari, A., & Teicher, M. H. (2008). Preliminary evidence for sensitive periods in the effect of childhood sexual abuse on regional brain development. *The Journal of Neuropsychiatry and Clinical Neurosciences, 20*, 292–301.

Bernard, K., Dozier, M., Bick, J., & Gordon, M. K. (2015). Intervening to enhance cortisol regulation among children at risk for neglect: Results of a randomized clinical trial. *Development and Psychopathology, 27*, 829–841. https://doi.org/10.1017/S095457941400073X

Bos, K. J., Fox, N., Zeanah, C. H., & Nelson, C. A. (2009). Effects of early psychosocial deprivation on the development of memory and executive function. *Frontiers in Behavioral Neuroscience, 3*(16). https://doi.org/10.3389/neuro.08.016.2009

Brassard, M. R., & Gelardo, M. S. (1987). Psychological maltreatment: The unifying construct in child abuse and neglect. *School Psychology Review, 16*, 127–136.

Bruce, J., Fisher, P. A., Pears, K. C., & Levine, S. (2009). Morning cortisol levels in preschool-aged foster children: Differential effects of maltreatment type. *Developmental Psychobiology: The Journal of the International Society for Developmental Psychobiology, 51*, 14–23.

Casanueva, C., Wilson, E., Smith, K., Dolan, M., Ringeisen, H., & Horne, B. (2012). *NSCAW II Wave 2 report: Child well-being* (OPRE Report No. 2012–38). Washington, DC: Office of Planning, Research and Evaluation, Administration for Children and Families, U.S. Department of Health and Human Services.

Cassidy, J., & Shaver, P. R. (Eds.). (2002). *Handbook of attachment: Theory, research, and clinical applications*. Rough Guides.

Chevignard, M. P., & Lind, K. (2014). Long-term outcome of abusive head trauma. *Pediatric Radiology, 44*, 548–558.

Christian, C. W., & Block, R. (2009). Abusive head trauma in infants and children. *Pediatrics, 123*, 1409–1411.

Christopolous, C., Bonvillian, J. D., & Crittenden, P. M. (1988). Maternal language input and child maltreatment. *Infant Mental Health, 9*, 272–286.

Chugani, H. T., Behen, M. E., Muzik, O., Juhász, C., Nagy, F., & Chugani, D. C. (2001). Local brain functional activity following early deprivation: A study of postinstitutionalized Romanian orphans. *NeuroImage, 14*, 1290–1301.

Cicchetti, D., & Carlson, V. (Eds.). (1989). *Child maltreatment: Theory and research on the causes and consequences of child abuse and neglect*. New York, NY: Cambridge University Press.

Cicchetti, D., & Rogosch, F. A. (2001). Diverse patterns of neuroendocrine activity in maltreated children. *Development and Psychopathology, 13*, 677–693.

Cicchetti, D., Rogosch, F. A., Gunnar, M. R., & Toth, S. L. (2010). The differential impacts of early physical and sexual abuse and internalizing problems on daytime cortisol rhythm in school-aged children. *Child Development, 81*, 252–269.

Cicchetti, D., Rogosch, F. A., Toth, S. L., & Sturge-Apple, M. L. (2011). Normalizing the development of cortisol regulation in maltreated infants through preventive interventions. *Development
and Psychopathology, 23*, 789–800. https://doi.org/10.1017/S0954579411000307

Clements, M. A., Reynolds, A. J., & Hickey, E. (2004). Site-level predictors of children's school
and social competence in the Chicago Child–Parent Centers. *Early Childhood Research
Quarterly, 19*, 273–296.

Cole, P. M., Martin, S. E., & Dennis, T. A. (2004). Emotion regulation as a scientific construct:
Methodological challenges and directions for child development research. *Child Development,
75*, 317–333. https://doi.org/10.1111/j.1467-8624.2004.00673.x

Cook, A., Spinazzola, J., Ford, J., Lanktree, C., Blaustein, M., Cloitre, M., ... Mallah, K. (2017).
Complex trauma in children and adolescents. *Psychiatric Annals, 35*, 390–398.

Coster, W. J., & Cicchetti, D. (1993). Research on the communicative development of maltreated
children: Clinical implications. *Topics in Language Disorders, 13*(4), 25–38.

Coster, W. J., Gersten, M. S., Beeghly, M., & Cicchetti, D. (1989). Communicative functioning in
maltreated toddlers. *Developmental Psychology, 25*, 1020–1029.

Courtois, C. A. (2008). Complex trauma, complex reactions: Assessment and treatment.
*Psychological Trauma Theory, Research, Practice and Policy, 1*, 86–100.

Crittenden, P. M., & DiLalla, D. L. (1988). Compulsive compliance: The development of an inhibitory coping strategy in infancy. *Journal of Abnormal Child Psychology, 16*, 585–599.

Culp, R. E., Watkins, R. V., Lawrence, H., Letts, D., Kelly, D. J., & Rice, M. L. (1991). Maltreated
children's language development: Abused, neglected, and abused and neglected. *First
Language, 11*, 377–389.

Cyr, C., Euser, E. M., Bakermans-Kranenburg, M. J., & Van Ijzendoorn, M. H. (2010). Attachment
security and disorganization in maltreating and high-risk families: A series of meta-analyses.
*Development and Psychopathology, 22*, 87–108. https://doi.org/10.1017/S0954579409990289

Danese, A., Caspi, A., Williams, B., Ambler, A., Sugden, K., Mika, J., ... Arseneault, L. (2011).
Biological embedding of stress through inflammation processes in childhood. *Molecular
Psychiatry, 16*, 244–246.

De Bellis, M. D., Hooper, S. R., Spratt, E. G., & Woolley, D. P. (2009). Neuropsychological findings in childhood neglect and their relationships to pediatric PTSD. *Journal of the International
Neuropsychological Society, 15*, 868–878.

De Bellis, M. D., Keshavan, M. S., Shifflett, H., Iyengar, S., Beers, S. R., Hall, J., & Moritz,
G. (2002). Brain structures in pediatric maltreatment-related posttraumatic stress disorder: A
sociodemographically matched study. *Biological Psychiatry, 52*, 1066–1078.

De Bellis, M. D., & Zisk, A. (2014). The biological effects of childhood trauma. *Child and
Adolescent Psychiatric Clinics, 23*, 185–222.

De Young, A. C., Kenardy, J. A., & Cobham, V. E. (2011). Trauma in early childhood: A neglected
population. *Clinical Child and Family Psychology Review, 14*, 231–250.

Dolan, M., Smith, K., Casanueva, C., Ringeisen, H., Dolan, M., Smith, K., ... Ringeisen, H.
(2011). *NSCAW II baseline report: Introduction to NSCAW II final report*. Washington, DC:
Office of Planning, Research and Evaluation, Administration for Children and Families,
U.S. Department of Health and Human Services.

Dozier, M., Manni, M., Gordon, M. K., Peloso, E., Gunnar, M. R., Stovall-McClough, K. C., ...
Levine, S. (2006). Foster children's diurnal production of cortisol: An exploratory study. *Child
Maltreatment, 11*, 189–197.

Drury, S. S., Theall, K., Gleason, M. M., Smyke, A. T., De Vivo, I., Wong, J. Y. Y., ... Nelson,
C. A. (2012). Telomere length and early severe social deprivation: Linking early adversity and
cellular aging. *Molecular Psychiatry, 17*, 719–727.

Dubowitz, H., & Black, M. (2002). Neglect of children's health. In J. Myers, L. Berliner, J. Briere,
C. Hendrix, & J. Carole (Eds.), *The APSAC handbook on child maltreatment* (2nd ed., pp. 269–
292). Thousand Oaks, CA: Sage.

Egeland, B., & Sroufe, L. A. (1981). Attachment and early maltreatment. *Child Development, 52*,
44–52.

Egeland, B., Sroufe, L. A., & Erickson, M. F. (1983). Developmental consequences of different patterns of maltreatment. *Child Abuse and Neglect, 7*, 459–469.

Egeland, B., Yates, T., Appleyard, K., & Van Dulmen, M. (2002). The long-term consequences of maltreatment in the early years: A developmental pathway model to antisocial behavior. *Children's Services: Social Policy, Research, and Practice, 5*, 249–260.

Eigsti, I., & Cicchetti, D. (2004). The impact of child maltreatment on expressive syntax at 60 months. *Developmental Science, 7*, 88–102.

Erickson, M. F., Egeland, B., & Pianta, R. (1989). The effects of maltreatment on the development of young children. In D. Cicchetti & V. Carlson (Eds.), *Child maltreatment: Theory and research on the causes and consequences of child abuse and neglect* (pp. 647–684). Boston, MA: Harvard University Press.

Evans, S. E., Davies, C., & DiLillo, D. (2008). Exposure to domestic violence: A meta-analysis of child and adolescent outcomes. *Aggression and Violent Behavior, 13*, 131–140.

Feldman, R., & Vengrober, A. (2011). Posttraumatic stress disorder in infants and young children exposed to war-related trauma. *Journal of the American Academy of Child & Adolescent Psychiatry, 50*, 645–658. https://doi.org/10.1016/j.jaac.2011.03.001

Finkelhor, D., Ormrod, R. K., & Turner, H. A. (2007). Poly-victimization: A neglected component in child victimization. *Child Abuse & Neglect, 31*, 7–26.

Finkelhor, D., Turner, H., Ormrod, R., & Hamby, S. (2009). Violence, crime, and exposure in a national sample of children and youth. *Pediatrics, 124*, 1411–1423.

Fishbein, D., Warner, T., Krebs, C., Trevarthen, N., Flannery, B., & Hammond, J. (2009). Differential relationships between personal and community stressors and children's neurocognitive functioning. *Child Maltreatment, 14*, 299–315.

Font, S. A., & Berger, L. M. (2015). Child maltreatment and children's developmental trajectories in early to middle childhood. *Child Development, 86*, 536–556. https://doi.org/10.1111/cdev.12322

Ford, J. D. (2017). Treatment implications of altered affect regulation and information processing following child maltreatment. *Psychiatric Annals, 35*, 410–419.

Ford, J. D., Racusin, R., Ellis, C. G., Daviss, W. B., Reiser, J., Fleischer, A., & Thomas, J. (2000). Child maltreatment, other trauma exposure, and posttraumatic symptomatology among children with oppositional defiant and attention deficit hyperactivity disorders. *Child Maltreatment, 5*, 205–217.

Fowler, P. J., Tompsett, C. J., Braciszewski, J. M., Jacques-Tiura, A. J., & Baltes, B. B. (2009). Community violence: A meta-analysis on the effect of exposure and mental health outcomes of children and adolescents. *Development and Psychopathology, 21*, 227–259.

Fox, L., Long, S. H., & Langlois, A. (1988). Patterns of language comprehension deficit in abused and neglected children. *Journal of Speech and Hearing Disorders, 53*, 239–244.

Gersten, M., Coster, W., Schneider-Rosen, K., Carlson, V., & Cicchetti, D. (1986). The socioemotional bases of communicative functioning: Quality of attachment, language development and early abuse. In M. Lamb, A. L. Brown, & B. Rogoff (Eds.), *Advances in developmental psychology* (pp. 105–151). Hillsdale, NJ: Lawrence Erlbaum.

Gleason, J. B., & Ratner, N. B. (2009). *The development of language*. Boston, MA: Pearson.

Goldsmith, H. H., Pollak, S. D., & Davidson, R. J. (2008). Developmental neuroscience perspectives on emotion regulation. *Child Development Perspectives, 2*, 132–140. https://doi.org/10.1111/j.1750-8606.2008.00055.x

Gonzalez, A. (2013). The impact of childhood maltreatment on biological systems: Implications for clinical interventions. *Paediatrics & Child Health, 18*, 415–418.

Gould, F., Clarke, J., Heim, C., Harvey, P. D., Majer, M., & Nemeroff, C. B. (2012). The effects of child abuse and neglect on cognitive functioning in adulthood. *Journal of Psychiatric Research, 46*, 500–506.

Hanson, J. L., Nacewicz, B. M., Sutterer, M. J., Cayo, A. A., Schaefer, S. M., Rudolph, K. D., … Davidson, R. J. (2015). Behavioral problems after early life stress: Contributions of the hippocampus and amygdala. *Biological Psychiatry, 77*, 314–323.

Herrenkohl, H. C., Herrenkohl, R. C., Toedter, L., & Yanushefski, A. M. (1984). Parent-child interactions in abusive and non-abusive families. *Journal of the American Academy of Child Psychiatry, 23*, 641–648.

Hesse, E., & Main, M. (2006). Frightened, threatening, and dissociative parental behavior in low-risk samples: Description, discussion, and interpretations. *Development and Psychopathology, 18*, 309–343. https://doi.org/10.1017/S0954579406060172

Holmes, C., Levy, M., Smith, A., Pinne, S., & Neese, P. (2015). A model for creating a supportive trauma-informed culture for children in preschool settings. *Journal of Child and Family Studies, 24*, 1650–1659.

Huang, H., Gundapuneedi, T., & Rao, U. (2012). White matter disruptions in adolescents exposed to childhood maltreatment and vulnerability to psychopathology. *Neuropsychopharmacology, 37*, 2693–2701.

Ivars, K., Nelson, N., Theodorsson, A., Theodorsson, E., Ström, J. O., & Mörelius, E. (2015). Development of salivary cortisol circadian rhythm and reference intervals in full-term infants. *PLoS One, 10*, e0129502. https://doi.org/10.1371/journal.pone.0129502

Jacobsen, H., Moe, V., Ivarsson, T., Wentzel-Larsen, T., & Smith, L. (2013). Cognitive development and social–emotional functioning in young foster children: A follow-up study from 2 to 3 years of age. *Child Psychiatry & Human Development, 44*, 666–677.

Jaffee, S., & Christian, C. (2014). The biological embedding of child abuse and neglect. *SRCD Social Policy Report, 28*, 3–19.

Jaffee, S. R., Caspi, A., Moffitt, T. E., & Taylor, A. (2004). Physical maltreatment victim to antisocial child: Evidence of an environmentally mediated process. *Journal of Abnormal Psychology, 113*, 44–55.

Jennissen, S., Holl, J., Mai, H., Wolff, S., & Barnow, S. (2016). Emotion dysregulation mediates the relationship between child maltreatment and psychopathology: A structural equation model. *Child Abuse & Neglect, 62*, 51–62.

Jones Harden, B., Buhler, A., & Jimenez Parra, L. (2016). Maltreatment in infancy: A developmental perspective on prevention and intervention. *Trauma, Violence, & Abuse, 17*, 366–386.

Jones Harden, B., Morrison, C., & Clyman, R. B. (2014). Emotion labeling among young children in foster care. *Early Education and Development, 25*, 1180–1197. https://doi.org/10.1080/10409289.2014.907694

Jones Harden, B., & Whittaker, J. V. (2011). The early home environment and developmental outcomes for young children in the child welfare system. *Children and Youth Services Review, 33*, 1392–1403. https://doi.org/10.1016/j.childyouth.2011.04.009

Jones, L. K., & Cureton, J. L. (2014). Trauma redefined in the DSM-5: Rationale and implications for counseling practice. *Professional Counselor: Research & Practice, 4*, 257–271.

Kelley, B. T., Thornberry, T. P., & Smith, C. A. (1997). *In the wake of childhood maltreatment.* Washington, DC: U.S. Department of Justice, Office of Justice Programs, Office of Juvenile Justice and Delinquency Prevention.

Kerker, B. D., Zhang, J., Nadeem, E., Stein, R. E., Hurlburt, M. S., Heneghan, A., … Horwitz, S. M. (2015). Adverse childhood experiences and mental health, chronic medical conditions, and development in young children. *Academic Pediatrics, 15*, 510–517.

Kim, J., & Cicchetti, D. (2010). Longitudinal pathways linking child maltreatment, emotion regulation, peer relations, and psychopathology. *Journal of Child Psychology and Psychiatry, 51*, 706–716.

Kim-Spoon, J., Cicchetti, D., & Rogosch, F. A. (2013). A longitudinal study of emotion regulation, emotion lability-negativity, and internalizing symptomatology in maltreated and nonmaltreated children. *Child Development, 84*, 512–527. https://doi.org/10.1111/j.1467-8624.2012.01857.x

Ko, S., Ford, J., Kassam-Adams, N., Berkowitz, S., Wilson, C., Wong, M., … Layne, C. (2008). Creating trauma-informed systems: Child welfare, education, first responders, health care, juvenile justice. *Professional Psychology: Research and Practice, 39*, 396–404.

Koenig, A. L., Cicchetti, D., & Rogosch, F. A. (2000). Child compliance/noncompliance and maternal contributors to internalization in maltreating and nonmaltreating dyads. *Child Development, 71*, 1018–1032.

Kurtz, P. D., Gaudin, J. M., Jr., Wodarski, J. S., & Howing, P. T. (1993). Maltreatment and the school-aged child: School performance consequences. *Child Abuse & Neglect, 17*, 581–589.

Lanier, P., Kohl, P. L., Raghavan, R., & Auslander, W. (2015). A preliminary examination of child well-being of physically abused and neglected children compared to a normative pediatric population. *Child Maltreatment, 20*, 72–79. https://doi.org/10.1177/1077559514557517

Leist, T., & Dadds, M. R. (2009). Adolescents' ability to read different emotional faces relates to their history of maltreatment and type of psychopathology. *Clinical Child Psychology and Psychiatry, 14*, 237–250.

Lemkin, A., Kistin, C. J., Cabral, H. J., Aschengrau, A., & Bair-Merritt, M. (2018). School connectedness and high school graduation among maltreated youth. *Child Abuse & Neglect, 75*, 130–138.

Leslie, L. K., Gordon, J. N., Ganger, W., & Gist, K. (2002). Developmental delay in young children in child welfare by initial placement type. *Infant Mental Health Journal, 23*, 496–516.

Levendosky, A. A., Okun, A., & Parker, J. G. (1995). Depression and maltreatment as predictors of social competence and social problem-solving skills in school-age children. *Child Abuse & Neglect, 19*, 1183–1195.

Love, J. M., Kisker, E. E., Ross, C., Constantine, J., Boller, K., Chazan-Cohen, R., & Vogel, C. (2005). The effectiveness of Early Head Start for 3-year-old children and their parents: Lessons for policy and programs. *Developmental Psychology, 41*, 885–901.

Ludwig, J., & Phillips, D. A. (2008). Long-term effects of Head Start on low-income children. *Annals of the New York Academy of Sciences, 1136*, 257–268.

Lyons-Ruth, K., & Block, D. (1996). The disturbed caregiving system: Relations among childhood trauma, maternal caregiving, and infant affect and attachment. *Infant Mental Health Journal, 17*, 257–275.

MacMillan, H. L., Georgiades, K., Duku, E. K., Shea, A., Steiner, M., Niec, A., … Walsh, C. A. (2009). Cortisol response to stress in female youths exposed to childhood maltreatment: Results of the youth mood project. *Biological Psychiatry, 66*, 62–68.

Maguire, S. A., Williams, B., Naughton, A. M., Cowley, L. E., Tempest, V., Mann, M. K., … Kemp, A. M. (2015). A systematic review of the emotional, behavioural and cognitive features exhibited by school-aged children experiencing neglect or emotional abuse. *Child: Care, Health and Development, 41*, 641–653.

Manly, J. T., Lynch, M., Oshri, A., Herzog, M., & Wortel, S. N. (2013). The impact of neglect on initial adaptation to school. *Child Maltreatment, 18*, 155–170. https://doi.org/10.1177/1077559513496144

Manso, J. M. M. (2009). Social adaptation and communicative competence in children in care. *Children and Youth Services Review, 31*, 642–648.

Manso, J. M. M., García-Baamonde, M. E., Alonso, M. B., & Barona, E. G. (2010). Pragmatic language development and educational style in neglected children. *Children and Youth Services Review, 32*, 1028–1034.

Manso, J. M. M., Sánchez, M. E. G. B., & Alonso, M. B. (2012). Morphosyntactic development and educational style of parents in neglected children. *Children and Youth Services Review, 34*, 311–315.

Masten, C. L., Guyer, A. E., Hodgdon, H. B., McClure, E. B., Charney, D. S., Ernst, M., … Monk, C. S. (2008). Recognition of facial emotions among maltreated children with high rates of post-traumatic stress disorder. *Child Abuse & Neglect, 32*, 139–153.

Maughan, A., & Cicchetti, D. (2002). Impact of child maltreatment and interadult violence on children's emotion regulation abilities and socioemotional adjustment. *Child Development, 73*, 1525–1542. https://doi.org/10.1111/1467-8624.00488

McCart, M. R., Smith, D. W., Saunders, B. E., Kilpatrick, D. G., Resnick, H., & Ruggiero, K. J. (2007). Do urban adolescents become desensitized to community violence? Data from a national survey. *American Journal of Orthopsychiatry, 77*, 434.

McFadyen, R. G., & Kitson, W. J. H. (1996). Language comprehension and expression among adolescents who have experienced childhood physical abuse. *Journal of Child Psychology Psychiatry & Allied Disciplines, 37*, 551–562.

Mehta, M. A., Golembo, N. I., Nosarti, C., Colvert, E., Mota, A., Williams, S. C., ... Sonuga-Barke, E. J. (2009). Amygdala, hippocampal and corpus callosum size following severe early institutional deprivation: The English and Romanian adoptees study pilot. *Journal of Child Psychology and Psychiatry, 50*, 943–951.

Mickelson, K. D., Kessler, R. C., & Shaver, P. R. (1997). Adult attachment in a nationally representative sample. *Journal of Personality and Social Psychology, 73*, 1092–1106.

Mills, R., Alati, R., O'Callaghan, M., Najman, J. M., Williams, G. M., Bor, W., & Strathearn, L. (2010). Child abuse and neglect and cognitive function at 14 years of age: Findings from a birth cohort. *Pediatrics, 127*, 4–10.

National Child Traumatic Stress Network. (2018). See various resources at www.nctsn.org and http://learn.nctsn.org.

National Research Council, & Institute of Medicine. (2009). *Preventing mental, emotional, and behavioral disorders among young people: Progress and possibilities.* Washington, DC: The National Academies Press. https://doi.org/10.17226/12480

National Scientific Council on the Developing Child. (2008). *The timing and quality of early experiences combine to shape brain architecture.* Harvard University, Center on the Developing Child.

Nelson, C. A., Zeanah, C. H., Fox, N. A., Marshall, P. J., Smyke, A. T., & Guthrie, D. (2007). Cognitive recovery in socially deprived young children: The Bucharest Early Intervention Project. *Science, 318*, 1937–1940.

Noll, J. G., Haralson, K. J., Butler, E. M., & Shenk, C. E. (2011). Childhood maltreatment, psychological dysregulation, and risky sexual behaviors in female adolescents. *Journal of Pediatric Psychology, 36*, 743–752.

Noll, J. G., Trickett, P. K., Long, J. D., Negriff, S., Susman, E. J., Shalev, I., ... Putnam, F. W. (2017). Childhood sexual abuse and early timing of puberty. *Journal of Adolescent Health, 60*, 65–71.

Norman, R. E., Byambaa, M., De, R., Butchart, A., Scott, J., & Vos, T. (2012). The long-term health consequences of child physical abuse, emotional abuse, and neglect: a systematic review and meta-analysis. *PLoS Medicine, 9*, e1001349.

O'Hara, M., Legano, L., Homel, P., Walker-Descartes, I., Rojas, M., & Laraque, D. (2015). Children neglected: Where cumulative risk theory fails. *Child Abuse & Neglect, 45*, 1–8.

Pears, K., & Fisher, P. A. (2005). Developmental, cognitive, and neuropsychological functioning in preschool-aged foster children: Associations with prior maltreatment and placement history. *Developmental and Behavioral Pediatrics, 26*, 112–122.

Perry, B. D. (2008). Child maltreatment: A neurodevelopmental perspective on the role of trauma and neglect in psychopathology. In T. P. Beauchaine & S. P. Hinshaw (Eds.), *Child and Adolescent Psychopathology* (pp. 93–128). Hoboken, NJ: Wiley.

Pine, D. S., Mogg, K., Bradley, B. P., Montgomery, L., Monk, C. S., McClure, E., ... Kaufman, J. (2005). Attention bias to threat in maltreated children: Implications for vulnerability to stress-related psychopathology. *American Journal of Psychiatry, 162*, 291–296.

Pollak, S. D. (2015). Multilevel developmental approaches to understanding the effects of child maltreatment: Recent advances and future challenges. *Development and Psychopathology, 27*, 1387–1397.

Pollak, S. D., Nelson, C. A., Schlaak, M. F., Roeber, B. J., Wewerka, S. S., Wiik, K. L., ... Gunnar, M. R. (2010). Neurodevelopmental effects of early deprivation in post-institutionalized children. *Child Development, 81*, 224–236. https://doi.org/10.1111/j.1467-8624.2009.01391.x

Robinson, L. R., Morris, A. S., Heller, S. S., Scheeringa, M. S., Boris, N. W., & Smyke, A. T. (2009). Relations between emotion regulation, parenting, and psychopathology in young mal-treated children in out of home care. *Journal of Child and Family Studies, 18*, 421–434.

Rogosch, F. A., Oshri, A., & Cicchetti, D. (2010). From child maltreatment to adolescent cannabis abuse and dependence: A developmental cascade model. *Development and Psychopathology, 22*, 883–897. https://doi.org/10.1017/S0954579410000520

Romano, E., Babchishin, L., Marquis, R., & Fréchette, S. (2015). Childhood maltreatment and educational outcomes. *Trauma, Violence, & Abuse, 16*, 418–437.

Romens, S. E., & Pollak, S. D. (2012). Emotion regulation predicts attention bias in maltreated children at-risk for depression. *Journal of Child Psychology and Psychiatry, 53*, 120–127. https://doi.org/10.1111/j.1469-7610.2011.02474.x

Sartori, R. F., Bandeira, P. F. R., Nobre, G. C., da Silva Ramalho, M. H., & Valentini, N. C. (2017). Associations between motor proficiency in children with history of maltreatment and living in social economically vulnerable. *Child Abuse & Neglect, 70*, 75–81.

Scheeringa, M. S., Myers, L., Putnam, F. W., & Zeanah, C. H. (2015). Maternal factors as modera-tors or mediators of PTSD symptoms in very young children: A two-year prospective study. *Journal of Family Violence, 30*, 633–642.

Scheeringa, M. S., Zeanah, C. H., Myers, L., & Putnam, F. W. (2003). New findings on alterna-tive criteria for PTSD in preschool children. *Journal of the American Academy of Child & Adolescent Psychiatry, 42*, 561–570.

Schneider-Rosen, K., & Cicchetti, D. (1984). The relationship between affect and cognition in maltreated infants: Quality of attachment and the development of visual self-recognition. *Child Development, 55*, 648–658.

Seltzer, L. J., Ziegler, T., Connolly, M. J., Prososki, A. R., & Pollak, S. D. (2014). Stress-induced elevation of oxytocin in maltreated children: Evolution, neurodevelopment, and social behav-ior. *Child Development, 85*, 501–512.

Shaffer, A., Huston, L., & Egeland, B. (2008). Identification of child maltreatment using prospec-tive and self-report methodologies: A comparison of maltreatment incidence and relation to later psychopathology. *Child Abuse & Neglect, 32*, 682–692.

Shalev, I., Moffitt, T. E., Sugden, K., Williams, B., Houts, R. M., Danese, A., … Caspi, A. (2013). Exposure to violence during childhood is associated with telomere erosion from 5 to 10 years of age: A longitudinal study. *Molecular Psychiatry, 18*, 576.

Sheridan, M., & Nelson, C. (2009). Neurobiology of fetal and infant development: Implications for infant mental health. In C. Zeanah (Ed.), *Handbook of infant mental health* (3rd ed., pp. 40–58). New York, NY: Guilford.

Sheridan, M. A., Fox, N. A., Zeanah, C. H., McLaughlin, K. A., & Nelson, C. A. (2012). Variation in neural development as a result of exposure to institutionalization early in childhood. *Proceedings of the National Academy of Sciences, 109*, 12927–12932.

Shirk, S. R. (1988). The interpersonal legacy of physical abuse of children. In M. Straus (Ed.), *Abuse and victimization across the lifespan*. Baltimore, MD: Johns Hopkins Press.

Shonkoff, J. P. (2010). Building a new biodevelopmental framework to guide the future of early childhood policy. *Child Development, 81*, 357–367. https://doi.org/10.1111/j.1467-8624.2009.01399.x

Shonkoff, J. P., Boyce, W. T., & McEwen, B. S. (2009). Neuroscience, molecular biology, and the childhood roots of health disparities: Building a new framework for health promotion and disease prevention. *JAMA, 301*, 2252–2259. https://doi.org/10.1001/jama.2009.754

Shonkoff, J. P., Garner, A. S., & Committee on Psychosocial Aspects of Child and Family Health, & Committee on Early Childhood, Adoption, and Dependent Care. (2011). The lifelong effects of early childhood adversity and toxic stress. *Pediatrics, 129*, e232–e246.

Slopen, N., Kubzansky, L. D., McLaughlin, K. A., & Koenen, K. C. (2013). Childhood adversity and inflammatory processes in youth: A prospective study. *Psychoneuroendocrinology, 38*, 188–200.

Spratt, E., Friedenberg, S., LaRosa, A., De Bellis, M., Macias, M., Summer, A., ... Brady, K. (2012). The effects of early neglect on cognitive language, and behavioral functioning in childhood. *Psychology, 3*, 175–182.

Stahmer, A. C., Hurlburt, M., Horwitz, S. M., Landsverk, J., Zhang, J., & Leslie, L. K. (2009). Associations between intensity of child welfare involvement and child development among young children in child welfare. *Child Abuse and Neglect, 33*, 598–611.

Stein, B. D., Jaycox, L. H., Kataoka, S. H., Wong, M., Tu, W., Elliott, M. N., & Fink, A. (2003). A mental health intervention for schoolchildren exposed to violence. *JAMA, 290*, 603–611. https://doi.org/10.1001/jama.290.5.603

Stock, C. D., & Fisher, P. A. (2006). Language delays among foster children: Implications for policy and practice. *Child Welfare, 85*, 445–461.

Sylvestre, A., Bussières, È. L., & Bouchard, C. (2016). Language problems among abused and neglected children: A meta-analytic review. *Child Maltreatment, 21*, 47–58.

Sylvestre, A., & Mérette, C. (2010). Language delay in severely neglected children: A cumulative or specific effect of risk factors? *Child Abuse & Neglect, 34*, 414–428.

Tamis-LeMonda, C. S., & Rodriguez, E. T. (2009). Parents' role in fostering young children's learning and language development. In *The encyclopedia on early childhood development*. Retrieved from http://www.child-encyclopedia.com/en-ca/language-development-literacy/according-to-experts/tamis-lemondarodriguez.html

Teicher, M. H., & Samson, J. A. (2013). Childhood maltreatment and psychopathology: A case for ecophenotypic variants as clinically and neurobiologically distinct subtypes. *American Journal of Psychiatry, 170*, 1114–1133.

Teicher, M. H., & Samson, J. A. (2016). Annual research review: Enduring neurobiological effects of childhood abuse and neglect. *Journal of Child Psychology and Psychiatry, 57*, 241–266.

Thompson, R. A. (1994). Emotion regulation: A theme in search of definition. *Monographs of the Society for Research in Child Development, 59*, 25–52.

Thompson, R. A. (2016). Early attachment and later development: Reframing the questions. In J. Cassidy & P. R. Shaver (Eds.), *Handbook of attachment* (3rd ed., pp. 330–348). New York, NY: Guilford.

Tottenham, N., Hare, T. A., Quinn, B. T., McCarry, T. W., Nurse, M., Gilhooly, T., ... Thomas, K. M. (2010). Prolonged institutional rearing is associated with atypically large amygdala volume and difficulties in emotion regulation. *Developmental Science, 13*, 46–61.

Trickett, P. K., Negriff, S., Ji, J., & Peckins, M. (2011). Child maltreatment and adolescent development. *Journal of Research on Adolescence, 21*, 3–20.

Trickett, P. K., Noll, J. G., Susman, E. J., Shenk, C. E., & Putnam, F. W. (2010). Attenuation of cortisol across development for victims of sexual abuse. *Development and Psychopathology, 22*, 165–175.

U.S. Department of Health and Human Services. (2005). *National survey of child and adolescent well-being: CPS sample component Wave 1 data analysis report*. Washington, DC: U.S. Government Printing Office.

U.S. Department of Health and Human Services. (2012a). *Information Memorandum: Promoting social-emotional well-being for children and youth receiving child welfare services. (ACYFCB-IM-12-04)*. Washington, DC: Author.

U.S. Department of Health and Human Services. (2012b). *Third grade follow-up to the Head Start Impact Study: Final report* (OPRE Report No. 2012–45). Retrieved from http://www.acf.hhs.gov/sites/default/files/opre/headstart report.pdf

U.S. Department of Health and Human Services. (2017). *Child maltreatment 2015*. Washington, DC: U.S. Government Printing Office.

U.S. Department of Justice. (2012). *Defending childhood: Report of the Attorney General's Task Force on Children Exposed to Violence*. Washington, DC: Author.

Van der Kolk, B. A. (2017). Developmental trauma disorder: Toward a rational diagnosis for children with complex trauma histories. *Psychiatric Annals, 35*, 401–408.

Van der Kolk, B. A., Roth, S., Pelcovitz, D., Sunday, S., & Spinazzola, J. (2005). Disorders of extreme stress: The empirical foundation of a complex adaptation to trauma. *Journal of Traumatic Stress, 18*, 389–399.

Wade, T. J., Bowden, J., & Sites, H. J. (2018). Child maltreatment and motor coordination deficits among preschool children. *Journal of Child & Adolescent Trauma, 11*, 159–162.

Waldinger, R. J., Schulz, M. S., Barsky, A. J., & Ahern, D. K. (2006). Mapping the road from childhood trauma to adult somatization: The role of attachment. *Psychosomatic Medicine, 68*, 129–135.

Whittle, S., Dennison, M., Vijayakumar, N., Simmons, J. G., Yücel, M., Lubman, D. I., ... Allen, N. B. (2013). Childhood maltreatment and psychopathology affect brain development during adolescence. *Journal of the American Academy of Child & Adolescent Psychiatry, 52*, 940–952.

Wodarski, J. S., Kurtz, P. D., Gaudin, J. M., Jr., & Howing, P. T. (1990). Maltreatment and the school-age child: Major academic, socioemotional, and adaptive outcomes. *Social Work, 35*, 506–513.

# Chapter 4
# Trauma, Self-Regulation, and Learning

Carlomagno C. Panlilio, Amanda Ferrara, and Leigha MacNeill

## 4.1 Introduction

Early experiences of maltreatment place students at a disadvantage upon school entry that often continues across elementary (Rouse & Fantuzzo, 2009) and secondary grades (Slade & Wissow, 2007). These experiences result in poor academic performance, which represent a different type of achievement gap that often cascades due to the developmental sequelae of maltreatment. With over four million referrals alleging maltreatment being reported to Child Protective Services in 2015 and representing an at-risk population of students (U.S. Department of Health and Human Services, 2017), it is important to identify malleable mechanisms that can be potential targets of intervention services within schools. Specifically, we identify self-regulation and self-regulated learning as two interrelated constructs that can help elucidate processes that result in these students' academic vulnerability.

We begin the chapter by conceptualizing self-regulation from a developmental science framework, outlining basic processes, examining the impact of maltreatment, and understanding how this in turn affects functioning within the school context. Next, we discuss self-regulated learning from the perspective of educational psychology and cover key components of the model along with how it relates to early adversity and self-regulation. Finally, we conclude the chapter with a brief discussion of our conceptual framework's implications for trauma-informed schools.

C. C. Panlilio (✉)
Department of Educational Psychology, Counseling, and Special Education,
The Pennsylvania State University, University Park, PA, USA
e-mail: panlilo@psu.edu

A. Ferrara · L. MacNeill
The Pennsylvania State University, State College, PA, USA

© Springer Nature Switzerland AG 2019
C. C. Panlilio (ed.), *Trauma-Informed Schools*, Child Maltreatment Solutions
Network, https://doi.org/10.1007/978-3-030-12811-1_4

## 4.2 Conceptualizing Self-Regulation

Self-regulation is broadly defined as the ability to initiate control processes such as shifting attention, effortful control, managing emotions, setting goals, monitoring one's own behaviors, and engaging positively with others (Borkowski, Chan, & Muthukrishna, 2000; Blair & Raver, 2015; Kopp, 2002; Murray & Kochanska, 2002; Thompson, 1994). Fox and Calkins (2003) proposed that an individual's ability to self-control is influenced by both intrinsic and extrinsic factors. Intrinsic factors include temperament, attention, effortful processes (e.g., response inhibition), and executive function processes, such as self-directedness and controlling processes before, during, and after a task. Extrinsic components consist of interactions with caregivers, peers, and environment.

### 4.2.1 Basic Processes

Researchers have categorized self-regulation behaviors into different domains: emotional, behavioral, and cognitive (Bell & Wolfe, 2004; Shields, Cicchetti, & Ryan, 1994). Emotion regulation is the process whereby individuals influence the emotions they experience and express, as well as where and when they express them (Gross, 1998). It also refers to processes that facilitate the individual's control of their own arousal and their ability to respond appropriately to emotional situations (Eisenberg & Fabes, 1992). Behavioral regulation typically consists of compliance with parents' directives and impulse control (Kopp, 1982; Kuczynski & Kochanska, 1995). Lastly, cognitive regulation is often comprised of volitional sustained attention, self-monitoring, and working memory (Bandura, 1991; Bell & Wolfe, 2004). The ability to concurrently regulate one's emotions, behavior, and cognition is a critical aspect of social competence for young children. These components of self-regulation provide a foundation upon which self-sufficiency and self-efficacy are later built (Trickett, 1998). Therefore, it is important to consider how these different aspects of regulation develop together and what factors contribute to, or disrupt, their development (Shields et al., 1994).

Generally, children with higher self-regulation are better able to address ongoing demands with a range of responses that are situationally appropriate and flexible. Higher levels of self-regulation have been related to greater social competence in the peer setting (Calkins, Gill, Johnson, & Smith, 1999). Children with lower levels of self-regulation may demonstrate heightened emotional reactivity or deficits in emotional experience or expression, such as restricted or inappropriate expressions and less empathic responding (Cole, Michel, & Teti, 1994). Lower levels of self-regulation have been linked to worse socioemotional functioning overall and more peer victimization (Eisenberg et al., 1995). The ability to self-regulate may help to explain the development of emotional and behavioral problems. For instance, girls with poor emotion regulation at age 2 had more chronic and clinical behavior problems between the ages of 2 and 5 (Hill, Degnan, Calkins, & Keane, 2006).

## 4.2.2 Self-Regulation in a Maltreating Context

The acquisition of early developmental abilities, including self-regulation, lays the groundwork for building later critical skills, such as making friends (Cicchetti & Schneider-Rosen, 1986). Disruptions in the development of effective self-regulation strategies early on may hinder later adaptive functioning (Shields et al., 1994). Experiencing maltreatment, for instance, may be one cause for these disruptions, as maltreated children have shown difficulties in their socioemotional functioning and ability to self-regulate (Cicchetti & Barnett, 1991; Cicchetti & Carlson, 1989). Traditionally, maltreatment research has focused on differences between maltreated children and non-maltreated children, but more recently, researchers have placed emphasis on how maltreated children develop psychopathology (Alink, Cicchetti, Kim, & Rogosch, 2009).

### 4.2.2.1 The Role of the Family: Emotional Security

In order to understand how maltreatment influences children's emerging self-regulation, researchers must first consider how this self-regulation is scaffolded by normative family contexts. Parents, specifically, play an important role in fostering adaptive self-regulatory strategies. Beginning in infancy, adults can engage and disengage the infant's attention to influence arousal: when an infant's attention is engaged, the infant may experience greater positive affect and arousal. A sensitive parent has the ability to know when to disengage infant attention in order to decrease too-high levels of arousal (Gottman, Katz, & Hooven, 1997). Through these interactions, infants learn the importance of attentional control as a strategy for self-regulation.

As children grow older, they shift from relying on external regulation (i.e., parents) to utilizing internal regulatory abilities that they have developed through the guidance of their parents (Rothbart & Bates, 1998). By 3 years of age, children demonstrate self-regulation across different situations and contexts, such as enhanced emotional understanding, planning and shifting attention to meet goals, and problem solving (Kopp, 2002; Murray & Kochanska, 2002). Sensitive parenting at 12 months of age, particularly autonomy support, has been related to better observed executive functioning at 26 months (Bernier, Carlson, & Whipple, 2010). Mothers' responsiveness with infants aged 22 months positively predicted child effortful control at 22 and 33 months (Kochanska, Murray, & Harlan, 2000).

One model to explain the role of family in the development of children's self-regulation is the emotional security theory of Davies and Cummings (1994), which suggests that children's emotional experiences mediate the relations between interparental conflict and children's adjustment. Children derive working models from important family relations, where if a child feels a sense of security in the family context, they are more likely to regulate their emotions effectively. Dysfunction in the family, however, may cause children to feel emotionally insecure, which places them at risk for the development of poor self-regulation. For example, children who have experienced maltreatment have demonstrated dysregulated emotion patterns in response to simulated interadult exchanges (Maughan & Cicchetti, 2002).

### 4.2.2.2  Maltreatment as a Disruptive Process

A large body of research demonstrates that parents play an important role in the development of children's self-regulation (Chang, Schwartz, Dodge, & McBride-Chang, 2003; Cole, Martin, & Dennis, 2004; Morris, Silk, Steinberg, Myers, & Robinson, 2007). Therefore, contexts of maltreatment are likely to hinder children's emerging regulatory abilities (Camras, Sachs-Alter, & Ribordy, 1996). First, maltreating parents create an emotional climate that fosters high arousal and vigilance on the part of the child, which can compromise the child's self-regulation system (Davies, Winter, & Cicchetti, 2006). Specifically, the overwhelming arousal that these children experience may decrease their ability to effectively process and manage their negative emotions (Kim & Cicchetti, 2010). While this pattern of regulatory behaviors may be considered maladaptive within normative environmental contexts, they are protective in dangerous ones. For instance, physically abused 8- to 11-year-old children during a computer task have shown faster responses to targets following angry faces than happy faces compared to non-maltreated children (Pollak & Tolley-Schell, 2003). Additionally, physical abuse by a family member has been positively associated with attention bias toward angry faces in 4- to 6-year-old children during a computer task. High angry bias also moderated the association between abuse and observed/reported child anxiety, as well as the association between harsh parenting and anxiety (Briggs-Gowan et al., 2015). These findings suggest that abusive parenting strategies heighten children's bias toward threats in their environment and potentially diminish children's abilities to regulate their negative affect.

Second, maltreated children are less able to rely on their caregivers for emotional availability and may not be exposed to adaptive emotion regulation strategies. The role of the caregiver, particularly early on in development, is to support children when they are angry or sad and teach them appropriate responses to these emotions. These behaviors are often compromised or absent in parents who maltreat their children (Kim & Cicchetti, 2010). Children who have been maltreated and who show difficulties in emotion regulation have also demonstrated greater reactive aggression (Shields & Cicchetti, 1998) and difficulties in social adjustment (Shields & Cicchetti, 2001). Maltreated children as young as 2 years of age were found to be more angry and noncompliant during a laboratory task than non-maltreated children when controlling for socioeconomic status. In preschool, these same maltreated children were more likely to be hyperactive and distractible, as well as to exhibit more negative affect (Erickson, Egeland, & Pianta, 1989). In their study of attention regulation in at-risk children, Shields and Cicchetti (1998) found that maltreated children exhibited more attention dysregulation than non-maltreated children, as well as more distractibility and overactivity and less ability to concentrate.

Some researchers posit that self-regulation mediates relations between maltreatment and child adjustment (e.g., Teisl & Cicchetti, 2008). Controlling for gender, maltreatment has been negatively associated with children's social competence, and self-regulatory ability mediated the relation between maltreatment status and peer competence (Shields et al., 1994). Children's risk for maltreatment has been linked to lower levels of self-regulation at 3 years of age, which in turn, predicted pre-academic skills and behavior problems at the age of 5 (Schatz, Smith, Borkowski, Whitman, & Keogh, 2008). For children who had experienced poor relatedness with their mother, maltreatment was associated with lower emotion regulation, which was subsequently related to children's internalizing and externalizing problems. This relation was not significant for children who had secure relationships with their mothers (Alink et al., 2009). Similarly, Kim and Cicchetti (2010) found that children who experienced neglect and sexual abuse had poorer emotion regulation, which was related to internalizing and externalizing problems. Additionally, children who experienced more than one type of maltreatment (e.g., sexual abuse, physical abuse, neglect) were more likely to be emotionally dysregulated.

Neurobiological changes in the brain may help to explain links between maltreatment and disruptions in the development of effective self-regulation. Genetic factors and the family environment contribute to early brain development (De Bellis, 2001). The first 2 years are particularly important due to the proliferation of synapses; individual experiences select which synaptic connections persist over time (Greenough & Black, 1992; Nelson, de Haan, & Thomas, 2006). Even in normative populations, differential patterns of frontal electroencephalography (EEG) asymmetry are linked to differences in infant parenting (Hane & Fox, 2006). Research suggests that early maltreatment influences neural structures and functioning, which may consequently affect the ability to manage or control one's behavioral or emotional experiences (Cicchetti & Tucker, 1994). Children who have been physically abused have shown increased P3b activity, an event-related potential component involved in attention allocation, in response to angry emotions during a computer task (Pollak & Tolley-Schell, 2003). The literature on stress physiology and the developmental sequelae of maltreatment provides evidence on structural and functional changes in the brain associated with self-regulation (see Jones Harden, Jimenez Parra, & Drouin Duncan, Chap. 3 in this volume). Despite the challenges associated with maltreatment and neurophysiological changes, however, researchers are also interested in examining how children develop adaptively under severe stress, as resilience is an important factor for implementing prevention, intervention, and policy (Cicchetti & Toth, 1992).

### 4.2.3   Self-Regulation in the School Context

In disrupting the development of self-regulation, maltreatment can negatively influence children's school performance, particularly as they transition from preschool to formal schooling (National Research Council and Institute of Medicine, 2000; Pianta, 2007). Self-regulation has been proposed as an important construct in understanding the development of children's school readiness (Eisenberg, Valiente, & Eggum, 2010), which is particularly important when viewed from a developmental psychobiological perspective and considering the neurophysiological sequelae of extremely stressful experiences (Blair & Raver, 2015) such as maltreatment. Differences in self-regulation capacity and school readiness are predictive of later academic performance such as math and literacy abilities (Blair & Razza, 2007; McWayne, Cheung, Wright, & Hahs-Vaughn, 2012; NRC & IOM, 2000), as well as educational attainment (Duncan & Magnuson, 2011).

Beyond preschool, older students with a history of maltreatment experience regulatory challenges across the emotional, behavioral, and cognitive domains of self-regulation, which relate to these later problems in academic performance. Therefore, self-regulation lends itself as an important mechanism that mediates early experiences of adversity and later academic outcomes (see Fig. 4.1).

Within the emotion regulation domain, students who have experienced maltreatment exhibit difficulty in being aware of their own emotions as well as those of others (Heleniak, Jenness, Vander Stoep, McCauley, & McLaughlin, 2016; Marusak, Martin, Etkin, & Thomason, 2015; Pollak & Sinha, 2002; Pollak & Tolley-Schell, 2003). This, in turn, relates to the inappropriate management or regulation of emotional responses (Kim & Cicchetti, 2010; Shields & Cicchetti, 2001). Without appropriate regulatory skills, students may fail to regulate their responses to emotional cues in the classroom. For example, students may respond in extreme ways to teachers' expressing negative emotions such as frustration and disappointment or be overwhelmed by intense positive expressions of excitement. In addition, social interactions with peers may be limited due to difficulties understanding others' emotions.

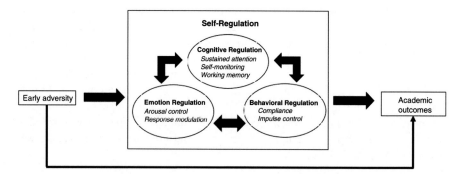

**Fig. 4.1** Self-regulation as a mediating mechanism between early adversity and later academic outcomes

Within the behavior regulation domain, students with a history of maltreatment often display externalizing or internalizing behaviors that are disruptive for learning (Heleniak et al., 2016; Hunt, Slack, & Berger, 2017). Externalizing behaviors are characterized as "acting out" and can include aggression, temper tantrums, problems with authority, and destruction of property. These symptoms are often disruptive for teachers' classroom management or students' capacity for engagement in learning-related activities. Students who exhibit internalizing symptoms of worry, fear, depression, or anxiety may become disengaged in the classroom and other learning-related activities due to preoccupation with managing these emotions.

Within the cognitive regulation domain, students who experience prior maltreatment are more likely to exhibit decreased executive functioning (Fay-Stammbach, Hawes, & Meredith, 2016; op den Kelder, Ensink, Overbeek, Maric, & Lindauer, 2017) in comparison to their peers. Executive functioning is an indicator of cognitive regulation that encompasses working memory, inhibition, and task shifting and is related to early literacy and mathematics achievement (Blair & Razza, 2007). Decreased cognitive regulatory capacity may also lead to problems with higher-order academic tasks such as following multipart instructions, reading comprehension, scientific reasoning, and mathematics computations.

Together, the emotional and behavioral responses outlined above represent automatic and reactive responses that are conceptualized as bottom-up processes related to stress physiology and emotional arousal (Blair, 2010; Blair & Ursache, 2010). Functionally, emotions serve to organize children's responses and provide meaning to these emotionally salient experiences, particularly those related to early adversity. Executive functions within the cognitive domain are top-down processes that have a bidirectional interaction with these bottom-up responses (Blair & Ursache, 2010). For students who experience maltreatment, observed emotional, behavioral, or cognitive challenges may reflect this organized pattern of responses that are adaptive in adverse environments. Although adaptive, these organized responses may not be optimal for learning and lead to challenges in the classroom environment that in turn lead to academic challenges.

Maltreated students often exhibit decreased grade point averages, standardized test scores, and homework completion rates when compared to their non-maltreated peers (Crozier & Barth, 2005; Leiter & Johnsen, 1994, 1997; Rouse & Fantuzzo, 2009; Slade & Wissow, 2007). Additionally, these already at-risk students demonstrate an increased number of school absences, a higher likelihood of dropping out of school, grade repetition, and a high involvement with special education (Leiter & Johnsen, 1994, 1997; Rouse & Fantuzzo, 2009). Further, Romano, Babchishin, Marquis, and Fréchette (2015) reported that children who have experienced maltreatment often exhibit mental health problems that are intertwined with these poor academic outcomes.

The mediating role of self-regulation (as seen in Fig. 4.1) in these outcomes is evident. For example, in a large, nationally representative sample of children who had contact with the Child Welfare System (CWS), being classified as emotionally dysregulated was associated with lower standardized test scores in reading and math by adolescence (Panlilio, Jones Harden, & Harring, 2017). Additionally, the authors found evidence that dysregulated emotional response problems persist across developmental periods. Specifically, children classified as emotionally dysregulated during their first contact with the CWS at age 4 were likely to remain classified as dysregulated across ages 5 and 6, which represents a transitional period from preschool to kindergarten and first grade. Schelble, Franks, and Miller (2010) found similar results wherein emotion dysregulation was associated with decreased academic resilience for students who had prior experiences of maltreatment. The normative transition to school is challenging even in the non-maltreated and typically developing population. Experiencing maltreatment and transitioning to school represent a difficult interactive experience that potentially places children at additional risk for poor academic outcomes by the time they transition to primary grades and continue beyond.

Given the multidimensional nature of self-regulation, the interactive processes across emotional, behavioral, and cognitive domains work in tandem to explain variability in academic performance for children who experienced maltreatment. For example, Manly, Lynch, Oshri, Herzog, and Wortel (2013) found that children's cognitive performance mediated the relationship between neglect severity and behavior regulation as well as first-grade academic performance. Additionally, children's maltreatment risk has been found to predict their cognitive and emotion regulation on a puzzle task, which in turn predicted their pre-academic skills (Schatz et al., 2008). For children in kindergarten and first grade, behavior and cognitive regulation mediated the relationship between foster placement and teacher-rated academic competence and special education placement (Pears, Fisher, Bruce, Kim, & Yoerger, 2010; Sanders & Fallon, 2018).

Taken together, the studies highlighted thus far provide evidence that self-regulation is an important mechanism to consider when linking early experiences of maltreatment with later academic performance. However, most of the evidence to date includes domain-general academic outcomes that are predominantly static and distal in nature. In order to understand how educators can provide the necessary instructional support for students within a trauma-informed framework, the inclusion of a conceptual model that promotes a more dynamic and proximal learning process is necessary. To address this, we propose the inclusion of a self-regulated learning model to guide the development of trauma-informed practices within the classroom.

### 4.2.4  Self-Regulated Learning

The dynamic interactions between maltreatment, self-regulation capacities, academic outcomes, and learning presented above are quite complex. One model that provides a unifying framework to account for this complexity is drawn from self-regulated learning (SRL). SRL is often defined as learning in which students are "metacognitively, motivationally, and behaviorally active participants in their own learning" (Zimmerman, 1990, p. 4). This view is in contrast with academic problems wherein students are more reactive and passive participants of the learning-related tasks or activities. SRL requires the use of higher-order executive functioning or complex cognitive processes (i.e., inferential reasoning, critical thinking, problem solving, and metacognition) within a top-down approach in order to maintain volitional and active participation in learning activities. Of particular interest is the construct of metacognition, which is defined as knowledge about one's own cognitive processes and other processes or outcomes related to cognition and learning (Flavell, 1979).

Metacognitive processes are important in monitoring one's own goals, progress toward those goals, strategy selection for goal attainment, flexibility to adjust as needed, and the evaluation of learning outcomes to inform future choices or effort (Zimmerman, 2008). For students who experienced prior maltreatment specifically, negative emotions related to early adversity and stress (e.g., bottom-up processes) may impede metacognitive awareness. Indeed, in a non-maltreated adult sample, perceived stress, anxiety, and depression were shown to be associated with metacognition (Spada, Nikcevic, Moneta, & Wells, 2008). In addition, as the model focuses on the active learning processes involved in an academic task, it necessarily involves cognitive or SRL engagement, defined by Cleary and Zimmerman (2012) as the use of cognitive strategies and regulatory processes, along with perceptions of interest and task values, which influence attention and immersion in the learning task.

According to Zimmerman's (2008) model, there are three dynamically related phases central to SRL: forethought, performance, and evaluation (see Fig. 4.2). Students begin in the forethought phase, in which they prepare to engage in an academic task. Successful engagement in this phase requires that students prepare for the task by setting goals and planning subsequent steps strategically. This, in turn, should influence students' motivation, defined as the energizing force to engage in a task. There are three components of motivation that are relevant in the forethought phase, particularly as these apply to students with a history of maltreatment: self-efficacy, task interest and value, and goal orientation (Zimmerman, 2008).

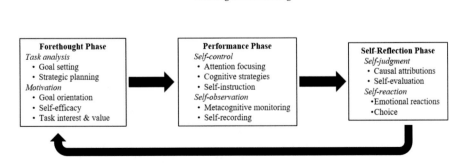

**Fig. 4.2** Phases and components of self-regulated learning

First, the degree to which students feel self-efficacious, or believe in their capacity to perform the task, can influence their level of motivation to engage in the learning-related task (Pajares, 1996). Unfortunately, perceptions of self-efficacy by students with a history of maltreatment may be inaccurate, leading to problems with academic functioning (Barnett, Vondra, & Shonk, 1996). Second, task interest and value depend on students' evaluations of how interesting they find the task to be, as well as the degree to which they believe the task will be beneficial to their immediate and long-term goals. Task interest and value are core components of achievement motivation and have been associated with student engagement in schools (Wang & Eccles, 2013; Wigfield & Eccles, 2000). Finally, goal orientation refers to students' beliefs about engagement in a learning-related task, which includes the broader constructs of mastery orientation and performance orientation. Mastery orientation refers to motivational tendencies to learn and master new skills, whereas performance orientation refers to the demonstration of skills in relation to others (Pintrich, 2003). Of these two broad orientations, mastery orientation has been associated with increased motivation and achievement in students (Ames, 1995; Pintrich, 2000). Taken together, these interrelated processes within the forethought phase are important in preparing a student for the performance phase where active engagement in the learning-related task will proceed.

The next phase of the SRL cycle is the performance phase, which includes the dimensions of self-control and self-observation. These two dimensions are important to consider in that the active volitional engagement in self-regulated learning is differentiated from more passive and automatized behaviors in the classroom and other learning-related contexts. Learners who are engaged in self-control can focus their attention, employ cognitive strategies, and engage in self-instruction toward the goal of acquiring knowledge or skill. Relatedly, self-observation involves metacognitive monitoring of performance, which allows for the shift in attention and selection of strategies as needed throughout the task in order to calibrate performance with goals from the forethought phase. Self-recording, such as taking notes or keeping a list of steps completed, can help to keep track, or be reminded, of progress toward the learning-related goal. Additionally, self-recording strategies can aid students in becoming more metacognitively aware of automatized responses that can support strategy selection. For example, if a student high on impulsivity was not aware of his or her problematic behaviors, asking him or her to begin tallying instances of said behaviors would increase awareness of when they occur. This level of awareness could then serve as a necessary step for the student to engage in self-reflection or self-observation around the precursors to said behaviors, as well as potential consequences of them. This in turn would facilitate metacognitive awareness of possible strategies, as well as awareness of the effectiveness of specific strategies that might decrease the occurrence of these problem behaviors.

Finally, when a task is complete, self-regulated students enter the self-reflection phase, in which they evaluate and react to the outcome of performance using two broad processes: self-judgment and self-reaction. Students who evaluate whether they attained their goal (set in the forethought phase) use self-judgment to examine the efficacy or effectiveness of their performance and to attribute success or failure to extrinsic or intrinsic factors, such as inaccurately or inappropriately attributing failure on a math test to a static trait (e.g., "I am not a math person") rather than ability, which is more malleable and subject to change through effort. Self-reaction is a process through which a learner examines her or his emotional reaction related to the outcome of the learning-related task, as well as how the outcome influences the selection of subsequent learning-related activities. For example, students who attribute failure on a math test to more trait-like reasons may not choose math-related courses in the future. This reaction can be adaptive or defensive, as students may choose to allow their performance to inform their planning and goal setting on their next task or believe that their performance was due to something outside of their control.

Although the SRL phases were presented in an ordered manner, SRL engagement may proceed from anywhere in the cycle. For example, a student may feel that a careful plan is unnecessary and begin on the task right away (i.e., reactive engagement). Through metacognitive monitoring, the student may realize that a broader goal is necessary to frame the learning-related task in order to develop a more appropriate plan to select specific strategies, which prompts movement from the performance phase to the forethought phase. Similarly, a student may feel that he or she does not have time to engage in self-reflection upon completion of a task, and so the student may think back to that task while creating a plan for a similar yet new task and use his or her judgments and reactions to inform that plan.

## 4.2.5  Maltreatment, Self-Regulation, and Self-Regulated Learning

Given the focus of this chapter on early experiences of maltreatment and related developmental sequelae, it is important to acknowledge individual differences in learning that may be related to variability in SRL engagement. Given the earlier discussion of maltreatment as a disruptive process for self-regulation development, compromised regulatory skills across cognitive, emotional, and behavioral domains may affect each of the SRL phases. This is a particularly salient point when considering the underlying neurobiological sequelae of maltreatment that relate to each domain of functioning, particularly in how bottom-up and top-down processes interact with goal-directed behaviors.

In the forethought phase, students may lack motivation to engage in the learning-related task due to the negative cascading effects of prior academic challenges. Motivational aspects of this phase may also be related to a mismatch in goal orientation between the student and a teacher. Specifically, students with early experiences of adversity might employ a goal that is more closely aligned with the need for emotional security rather than mastery- or performance-oriented goals. Within the performance phase, compromised top-down processes may cause students to rely more on automatic and reactive bottom-up processes such as externalizing or internalizing behaviors. For example, a perceived threat in the classroom context may engage a student's bottom-up process to alert and orient attention toward this threat (e.g., Pollak & Tolley-Schell, 2003) with an accompanying aggressive response, hijacking any effortful attentional and behavioral control through top-down executive processes. These emotionally reactive processes may preclude students from engaging in more reflective and intentional strategy selection, which also compromises metacognitive awareness and learning. Finally, students with a history of maltreatment may exhibit problems in the self-reflection phase. For example, Brown and Kolko (1999) found that children with histories of abuse subscribed to abuse-specific and general attributional styles (e.g., self-oriented and other-oriented) that were associated with internalizing and externalizing symptoms. Students with abuse histories also exhibited problems with self-evaluation: maltreated students in younger grades tended to exaggerate their positive self-evaluation beyond a self-enhancement bias typically exhibited by young children (Vondra, Barnett, & Cicchetti, 1989). The authors added that by the elementary grades, maltreated students exhibited more negative self-evaluation of their abilities compared with community samples. Taken together, these connections highlight the importance of further examining the role that SRL, in addition to self-regulatory capacities, plays in explaining variability in academic performance for children who experience maltreatment.

### 4.2.6   Conclusion and Future Directions

Early experiences of adversity, particularly maltreatment, have been associated with academic vulnerability for students. It is therefore imperative that child-serving systems, especially schools, engage with students and families to promote academic success. In order to do so, mechanisms that are salient intervention targets must be identified in order to attenuate the impact of trauma. Self-regulation and self-regulated learning are two interrelated processes that show promise as malleable mechanisms that explain the link between early adverse experiences and later academic challenges. These important developmental and learning processes should be considered within a trauma-informed school framework due to their potential in explaining proximal and dynamic learning processes for students. Moreover, these processes can be incorporated into classroom-level interventions that provide educators with targeted processes to support, guide, and promote learning.

According to the Substance Abuse and Mental Health Services Administration (SAMHSA), the six key principles of a general trauma-informed framework are safety; trustworthiness and transparency; peer support; collaboration and mutuality; empowerment, voice, and choice; and cultural, historical, and gender issues. Within schools, trauma-informed approaches often employ a multitier method of service delivery that incorporates a trauma lens in understanding and responding to students who have experienced prior adversity (Phifer & Hull, 2016). Despite the growing trend of schools adopting trauma-informed frameworks that incorporate self-regulatory domains of functioning, consideration of concurrent dynamic processes of learning is missing from the majority of trauma-informed practices in schools (for program examples, see Chafouleas, Johnson, Overstreet, & Santos, 2016). Moreover, evaluations of current school-based trauma-informed practices are needed to understand what fidelity standards are being followed (e.g., SAMHSA principles or more specific trauma-informed models), to what degree these programs are effective, and the potential iatrogenic effects, as well as to explicate more proximal learning mechanisms related to early adversity and academic outcomes.

To address the need for connecting adversity, self-regulation, and learning, future work should examine a unified framework that incorporates self-regulation and self-regulated learning in order to test how this broader model, along with individual components, might account for variability in academic outcomes for these vulnerable students. Next, there needs to be a shift in how we conceptualize academic outcomes that would incorporate dynamic and proximal learning processes (e.g., engagement in the SRL cycle to learn specific learning-related tasks) into the current conceptualization of static and distal outcomes (e.g., graduation rates, GPA, grade retention) compromised by early adversity. Additionally, purposeful integration of socioemotional competence with cognitive processes that are impacted by early maltreatment experiences should be considered within a trauma-informed framework. More individual difference factors, such as temperament, higher-order executive functions, and academic socialization practices in homes, should also be considered in understanding variability in regulatory processes and academic outcomes. Next, domain-specific (e.g., mathematics, science, social studies) learning activities should be incorporated into the current domain-general academic outcomes of interest. Finally, developmental trends in these specific mechanisms must be considered. Given the importance of school as a developmental and learning context for students who have experienced early maltreatment, a closer look into these malleable mechanisms is warranted to provide supports that could potentially shift student development and learning trajectories in a more positive direction.

# References

Alink, L. R. A., Cicchetti, D., Kim, J., & Rogosch, F. A. (2009). Mediating and moderating processes in the relation between maltreatment and psychopathology: Mother-child relationship quality and emotion regulation. *Journal of Abnormal Child Psychology, 37*, 831–843. https://doi.org/10.1007/s10802-009-9314-4

Ames, C. (1995). Achievement goals, motivational climate, and motivational processes. In G. C. Roberts (Ed.), *Motivation in sport and exercise* (pp. 161–176). Champaign, IL: Human Kinetics Books.

Bandura, A. (1991). Social cognitive theory of self-regulation. *Organizational Behavior and Human Decision Processes, 50*, 248–287. https://doi.org/10.1016/0749-5978(91)90022-L

Barnett, D., Vondra, J. I., & Shonk, S. M. (1996). Self-perceptions, motivation, and school functioning of low-income maltreated and comparison children. *Child Abuse & Neglect, 20*, 397–410.

Bell, M. A., & Wolfe, C. D. (2004). Emotion and cognition: An intricately bound developmental process. *Child Development, 75*, 366–370. https://doi.org/10.1111/j.1467-8624.2004.00679.x

Bernier, A., Carlson, S. M., & Whipple, N. (2010). From external regulation to self-regulation: Early parenting precursors of young children's executive functioning. *Child Development, 81*, 326–339. https://doi.org/10.1111/j.1467-8624.2009.01397.x

Blair, C. (2010). Stress and the development of self-regulation in context. *Child Development Perspectives, 4*, 181–188. https://doi.org/10.1111/j.1750-8606.2010.00145.x

Blair, C., & Raver, C. C. (2015). School readiness and self-regulation: A developmental psychobiological approach. *Annual Review of Psychology, 66*, 711–731. https://doi.org/10.1146/annurev-psych-010814-015221

Blair, C., & Razza, R. P. (2007). Relating effortful control, executive function, and false belief understanding to emerging math and literacy ability in kindergarten. *Child Development, 78*(2), 647–663.

Blair, C., & Ursache, A. (2010). A bidirectional model of executive functions and self-regulation. In K. D. Vohs & R. F. Baumeister (Eds.), *Handbook of self-regulation: Research, theory, and applications* (2nd ed., pp. 300–320). New York, NY: Guilford.

Borkowski, J. G., Chan, L. K., & Muthukrishna, N. (2000). A process oriented model of metacognition: Links between motivation and executive functioning. In G. Schraw & J. Impara (Eds.). *Issues in the measurement of metacognition* (pp. 1–42). Lincoln, NE: Buros Institute of Mental Measurements, University of Nebraska

Briggs-Gowan, M. J., Pollak, S. D., Grasso, D., Voss, J., Mian, N. D., Zobel, E., ... Pine, D. S. (2015). Attention bias and anxiety in young children exposed to family violence. *Journal of Child Psychology and Psychiatry, 56*(11), 1194–1201. https://doi.org/10.1111/jcpp.12397

Brown, E. J., & Kolko, D. J. (1999). Child victims' attributions about being physically abused: An examination of factors associates with symptom severity. *Journal of Abnormal Child Psychology, 27*, 311–322.

Calkins, S. D., Gill, K. L., Johnson, M. C., & Smith, C. L. (1999). Emotional reactivity and emotional regulation strategies as predictors of social behavior with peers during toddlerhood. *Social Development, 8*(3), 310–334. https://doi.org/10.1111/1467-9507.00098

Camras, L. A., Sachs-Alter, E., & Ribordy, S. C. (1996). Emotion understanding in maltreated children: Recognition of facial expressions and integration with other emotion cues. In *Emotional development in atypical children* (pp. 203–225). Hillsdale, NJ: Lawrence Erlbaum Associates, Inc.

Chafouleas, S. M., Johnson, A. H., Overstreet, S., & Santos, N. M. (2016). Toward a blueprint for trauma-informed service delivery in schools. *School Mental Health, 8*, 144–162. https://doi.org/10.1007/s12310-015-9166-8

Chang, L., Schwartz, D., Dodge, K. A., & McBride-Chang, C. (2003). Harsh parenting in relation to child emotion regulation and aggression. *Journal of Family Psychology, 17*(4), 598–606. https://doi.org/10.1037/0893-3200.17.4.598

Cicchetti, D., & Barnett, D. (1991). Attachment organization in preschool aged maltreated children. *Development and Psychopathology, 3*, 397–411.

Cicchetti, D., & Carlson, V. (1989). *Child maltreatment: Theory and research on the causes and consequences of child abuse and neglect*. New York, NY: Cambridge University Press.

Cicchetti, D., & Schneider-Rosen, K. (1986). An organizational approach to childhood depression. In M. Rutter, C. Izard, & P. B. Read (Eds.), *Depression in young people: Developmental and clinical perspectives* (pp. 71–134). New York, NY: Guilford Press.

Cicchetti, D., & Toth, S. L. (1992). The role of developmental theory in prevention and intervention. *Development and Psychopathology, 4*, 489–493. https://doi.org/10.1017/S0954579400004831

Cicchetti, D., & Tucker, D. (1994). Development and self-regulatory structures of the mind. *Development and Psychopathology, 6*, 533–549. https://doi.org/10.1017/S0954579400004673

Cleary, T. J., & Zimmerman, B. J. (2012). A cyclical self-regulatory account of student engagement: Theoretical foundations and applications. In S. L. Christenson, A. Reschly, & C. Wylie (Eds.), *Handbook of research on student engagement* (pp. 237–257). Boston, MA: Springer.

Cole, P. M., Martin, S. E., & Dennis, T. A. (2004). Emotion regulation as a scientific construct: Methodological challenges and directions for child development research. *Child Development, 75*, 317–333. https://doi.org/10.1111/j.1467-8624.2004.00673.x

Cole, P. M., Michel, M. K., & Teti, L. O. (1994). The development of emotion regulation and dysregulation: A clinical perspective. *Monographs of the Society for Research in Child Development, 59*, 73–100.

Crozier, J. C., & Barth, R. P. (2005). Cognitive and academic functioning in maltreated children. *Children and Schools, 27*(4), 197–206. https://doi.org/10.1093/cs/27.4.197

Davies, P. T., & Cummings, E. M. (1994). Marital conflict and child adjustment: An emotional security hypothesis. *Psychological Bulletin, 116*, 387–411.

Davies, P. T., Winter, M. A., & Cicchetti, D. (2006). The implications of emotional security theory for understanding and treating childhood psychopathology. *Development and Psychopathology, 18*, 707–735. https://doi.org/10.1017/S0954579406060354

De Bellis, M. D. (2001). Developmental traumatology: The psychobiological development of maltreated children and its implications for research, treatment, and policy. *Development and Psychopathology, 13*, 539–564.

Duncan, G. J., & Magnuson, K. (2011). The nature and impact of early achievement skills, attention skills, and behavior problems. In G. J. Duncan & R. J. Murnane (Eds.), *Whither opportunity: Rising inequality, schools, and children's life chances* (pp. 47–69). New York, NY: Russell Sage.

Eisenberg, N., & Fabes, R. A. (1992). *Emotion and its regulation in early development*. San Francisco, CA: Jossey-Bass.

Eisenberg, N., Fabes, R. A., Murphy, B., Maszk, P., Smith, M., & Karbon, M. (1995). The role of emotionality and regulation in children's social functioning: A longitudinal study. *Child Development, 66*, 1360–1384. https://doi.org/10.1111/j.1467-8624.1995.tb00940.x

Eisenberg, N., Valiente, C., & Eggum, N. D. (2010). Self-regulation and school readiness. *Early Education and Development, 21*, 681–698.

Erickson, M. F., Egeland, B., & Pianta, R. (1989). The effects of maltreatment on the development of young children. In D. Cicchetti & V. Carlson (Eds.), *Child maltreatment: Theory and research on the causes and consequences of child abuse and neglect* (pp. 647–684). New York, NY: Cambridge University Press.

Fay-Stammbach, T., Hawes, D. J., & Meredith, P. (2016). Child maltreatment and emotion socialization: Associations with executive function in the preschool years. *Child Abuse and Neglect, 64*(1), 1–12.

Flavell, J. H. (1979). Metacognition and cognitive monitoring: A new area of cognitive-developmental inquiry. *American Psychologist, 34*, 906–911.

Fox, N. A., & Calkins, S. D. (2003). The development of self-control of emotion: Intrinsic and extrinsic influences. *Motivation and Emotion, 27*, 7–26. https://doi.org/10.1023/A:1023622324898

Gottman, J., Katz, L., & Hooven, C. (1997). *Meta-emotion*. Hillsdale, NJ: Erlbaum.

Greenough, W. T., & Black, J. E. (1992). Induction of brain structure by experience: Substrates for cognitive development. In M. R. Gunnar & C. A. Nelson (Eds.), *Developmental behavioral neuroscience: The Minnesota symposia on child psychology* (Vol. 24, pp. 155–200). Hillsdale, NJ: Erlbaum.

Gross, J. J. (1998). The emerging field of emotional regulation: An integrative review. *Review of General Psychology, 2*, 271–299.

Hane, A. A., & Fox, N. A. (2006). Ordinary variations in maternal caregiving influence human infants' stress reactivity. *Psychological Science, 17*, 550–556. https://doi.org/10.1111/j.1467-9280.2006.01742.x

Heleniak, C., Jenness, J., Vander Stoep, A., McCauley, E., & McLaughlin, K. (2016). Childhood maltreatment exposure and disruptions in emotion regulation: A transdiagnostic pathway to adolescent internalizing and externalizing psychopathology. *Cognitive Therapy and Research, 40*(3), 394–415.

Hill, A. L., Degnan, K. A., Calkins, S. D., & Keane, S. P. (2006). Profiles of externalizing behavior problems for boys and girls across preschool: The roles of emotion regulation and inattention. *Developmental Psychology, 42*, 913–928. https://doi.org/10.1037/0012-1649.42.5.913

Hunt, T. K. A., Slack, K. S., & Berger, L. M. (2017). Adverse childhood experiences and behavioral problems in middle childhood. *Child Abuse and Neglect, 67*(1), 391–402.

Kim, J., & Cicchetti, D. (2010). Longitudinal pathways linking child maltreatment, emotion regulation, peer relations, and psychopathology. *Journal of Child Psychology and Psychiatry, 51*(6), 706–716.

Kochanska, G., Murray, K. T., & Harlan, E. T. (2000). Effortful control in early childhood: Continuity and change, antecedents, and implications for social development. *Developmental Psychology, 36*, 220–232. https://doi.org/10.1037/0012-1649.36.2.220

Kopp, C. B. (1982). Antecedents of self-regulation: A developmental perspective. *Developmental Psychology, 18*, 199–214.

Kopp, C. B. (2002). Commentary: The codevelopments of attention and emotion regulation. *Infancy, 3*, 199–208. https://doi.org/10.1207/S15327078IN0302_5

Kuczynski, L., & Kochanska, G. (1995). Function and content of maternal demands: Developmental significance of early demands for competent action. *Child Development, 66*, 616–628. https://doi.org/10.1111/j.1467-8624.1995.tb00893.x

Leiter, J., & Johnsen, M. C. (1994). Child maltreatment and school performance. *American Journal of Education, 102*(2), 154–189. https://doi.org/10.2307/1163250

Leiter, J., & Johnsen, M. C. (1997). Child maltreatment and school performance declines: An event-history analysis. *American Educational Research Journal, 34*(3), 563–589. https://doi.org/10.2307/1163250

Manly, J. T., Lynch, M., Oshri, A., Herzog, M., & Wortel, S. N. (2013). The impact of neglect on initial adaption to school. *Child Maltreatment, 18*(3), 155–170.

Marusak, H. A., Martin, K. R., Etkin, A., & Thomason, M. E. (2015). Childhood trauma exposure disrupts automatic regulation of emotional processing. *Neuropsychopharmacology, 40*(1), 1250–1258.

Maughan, A., & Cicchetti, D. (2002). Impact of child maltreatment and interadult violence on children's emotion regulation abilities and socioemotional adjustment. *Child Development, 73*, 1525–1542. https://doi.org/10.1111/1467-8624.00488

McWayne, C. M., Cheung, K., Wright, L. E. G., & Hahs-Vaughn, D. L. (2012). Patterns of school readiness among Head Start children: Meaningful within-group variability during the transition to kindergarten. *Journal of Educational Psychology, 104*, 862–878.

Morris, A. S., Silk, J. S., Steinberg, L., Myers, S. S., & Robinson, L. R. (2007). The role of the family context in the development of emotion regulation. *Social Development, 16*, 361–388. https://doi.org/10.1111/j.1467-9507.2007.00389.x

Murray, K. T., & Kochanska, G. (2002). Effortful control: Factor structure and relation to externalizing and internalizing behaviors. *Journal of Abnormal Child Psychology, 30*, 503–514. https://doi.org/10.1023/A:1019821031523

National Research Council and Institute of Medicine. (2000). In J. P. Shonkoff & D. A. Phillips (Eds.), *From neurons to neighborhoods: The science of early childhood development.* Washington, DC: National Academy Press.

Nelson, C. A., de Haan, M., & Thomas, K. M. (2006). *Neuroscience of cognitive development: The role of experience and the developing brain.* Hoboken, NJ: Wiley.

op den Kelder, R., Ensink, J. B. M., Overbeek, G., Maric, M., & Lindauer, R. J. L. (2017). Executive function as a mediator in the link between single or complex trauma and posttraumatic stress in children and adolescents. *Quality of Life Research, 26*(7), 1687–1696.

Pajares, F. (1996). Self-efficacy beliefs in academic settings. *Review of Educational Research, 66*(4), 543–578.

Panlilio, C. C., Jones Harden, B., & Harring, J. (2017). School readiness of maltreated preschoolers and later school achievement: The role of emotion regulation, language, and context. *Child Abuse & Neglect, 75*, 82–91. https://doi.org/10.1016/j.chiabu.2017.06.004

Pears, K. C., Fisher, P. A., Bruce, J., Kim, H. K., & Yoerger, K. (2010). Early elementary school adjustment of maltreated children in foster care: The roles of inhibitory control and caregiver involvement. *Child Development, 81*(5), 1550–1564.

Phifer, L. W., & Hull, R. (2016). Helping students heal: Observations of trauma-informed practices in the schools. *School Mental Health, 8*, 201–205. https://doi.org/10.1007/s12310-016-9183-2

Pianta, R. C. (2007). Early education in transition. In R. C. Pianta, M. J. Cox, & K. L. Snow (Eds.), *School readiness & the transition to kindergarten in the era of accountability* (pp. 3–10). Baltimore, MD: Paul H. Brookes Publishing.

Pintrich, P. R. (2000). Multiple goals, multiple pathways: The role of goal orientation in learning and achievement. *Journal of Educational Psychology, 92*(3), 544–555.

Pintrich, P. R. (2003). Motivation and classroom learning. In I. B. Weiner (Ed.), *Handbook of psychology* (pp. 103–122). Hoboken, NJ: Wiley & Sons, Inc.

Pollak, S. D., & Sinha, P. (2002). Effects of early experience on children's recognition of facial displays of emotion. *Developmental Psychology, 38*(5), 784–791. https://doi.org/10.1037/0012-1649.38.5.784

Pollak, S. D., & Tolley-Schell, S. A. (2003). Selective attention to facial emotion in physically abused children. *Journal of Abnormal Psychology, 112*(3), 323–338. https://doi.org/10.1037/0021-843X.112.3.323

Romano, E., Babchishin, L., Marquis, R., & Fréchette, S. (2015). Childhood maltreatment and educational outcomes. *Trauma, Violence, & Abuse, 16*(4), 418–437. https://doi.org/10.1177/1524838014537908

Rothbart, M. K., & Bates, J. E. (1998). Temperament. In W. Damon (Series Ed.) & N. Eisenberg (Vol. Ed.), *Handbook of child psychology: Vol. 3. Social, emotional and personality development* (5th ed., pp. 105–176). New York, NY: Wiley.

Rouse, H. L., & Fantuzzo, J. W. (2009). Multiple risks and educational well being: A population-based investigation of threats to early school success. *Early Childhood Research Quarterly, 24*(1), 1–14. https://doi.org/10.1016/j.ecresq.2008.12.001

Sanders, J. E., & Fallon, B. (2018). Child welfare involvement and academic difficulties: Characteristics of children, families, and households involved with child welfare and experiencing academic difficulties. *Children and Youth Services Review, 86*(1), 98–109.

Schatz, J. N., Smith, L. E., Borkowski, J. G., Whitman, T. L., & Keogh, D. A. (2008). Maltreatment risk, self-regulation, and maladjustment in at-risk children. *Child Abuse and Neglect, 32*(10), 972–982. https://doi.org/10.1016/j.chiabu.2008.09.001

Schelble, J. L., Franks, B. A., & Miller, M. D. (2010). Emotion dysregulation and academic resilience in maltreated children. *Child and Youth Care Forum, 39*(4), 289–303. https://doi.org/10.1007/s10566-010-9105-7

Shields, A., & Cicchetti, D. (1998). Reactive aggression among maltreated children: The contributions of attention and emotion dysregulation. *Journal of Clinical Child Psychology, 27*, 381–395. https://doi.org/10.1207/s15374424jccp2704_2

Shields, A., & Cicchetti, D. (2001). Parental maltreatment and emotion dysregulation as risk factors for bullying and victimization in middle childhood. *Journal of Clinical Child and Adolescent Psychology, 30*(3), 349–363.

Shields, A. M., Cicchetti, D., & Ryan, R. M. (1994). The development of emotional and behavioral self-regulation and social competence among maltreated school-age children. *Development and Psychopathology, 6*, 57–75. https://doi.org/10.1017/S0954579400005885

Slade, E. P., & Wissow, L. S. (2007). The influence of childhood maltreatment on adolescents' academic performance. *Economics of Education Review, 26*(5), 604–614. https://doi.org/10.1016/j.econedurev.2006.10.003

Spada, M. M., Nikcevic, A. V., Moneta, G. B., & Wells, A. (2008). Metacognition, perceived stress, and negative emotion. *Personality and Individual Differences, 44*, 1172–1181.

Teisl, M., & Cicchetti, D. (2008). Physical abuse, cognitive and emotional processes, and aggressive/disruptive behavior problems. *Social Development, 17*, 1–23. https://doi.org/10.1111/j.1467-9507.2007.00412.x

Thompson, R. A. (1994). Emotion regulation: A theme in search of definition. *Monographs of the Society for Research in Child Development, 59*, 25–52.

Trickett, P. K. (1998). Multiple maltreatment and the development of self and emotion regulation. *Journal of Aggression, Maltreatment & Trauma, 2*, 171–187. https://doi.org/10.1300/J146v02n01_10

U.S. Department of Health and Human Services. (2017). *Child Maltreatment 2015*. Washington, DC: U.S. Government Printing Office.

Vondra, J., Barnett, D., & Cicchetti, D. (1989). Perceived and actual competence among maltreated and comparison school children. *Development and Psychopathology, 1*, 237–255.

Wang, M., & Eccles, J. S. (2013). School context, achievement motivation, and academic engagement: A longitudinal study of school engagement using a multidimensional perspective. *Learning and Instruction, 28*, 12–23.

Wigfield, A., & Eccles, J. S. (2000). Expectancy-value theory of achievement motivation. *Contemporary Educational Psychology, 25*, 68–81.

Zimmerman, B. J. (1990). Self-regulated learning and academic achievement: An overview. *Educational Psychologist, 25*(1), 3–17. https://doi.org/10.1207/s15326985ep2501

Zimmerman, B. J. (2008). Investigating self-regulation and motivation: Historical background, methodological developments, and future prospects. *American Educational Research Journal, 45*(1), 166–183. https://doi.org/10.3102/0002831207312909

# Chapter 5
# Maltreatment as a Wicked Problem: Implications for Educational Settings

Susan Stone

## 5.1 Introduction

This chapter draws on the concept of a "wicked problem" (Rittel & Webber, 1973) to frame the social problem of child maltreatment and ultimately to consider roles of schools and other child-serving systems of care in responding to it. After defining the contours and dynamics of wicked problems, the chapter will selectively review literature on maltreatment and child welfare system involvement, with specific attention to its relationship to student academic difficulty and the evidence base on prevention and intervention with maltreated children. Because maltreated children often are identified and receive services through various systems of care, key features of these systems will be highlighted, with a focus on surfacing organizational and institutional features, particularly within educational settings, that will likely shape response to this subgroup. Drawing on recent scholarship regarding wicked problems, this chapter discusses a set of options that might be considered to help schools better target prevention and intervention efforts to children who have experienced maltreatment.

## 5.2 Conceptualizing Wicked Problems

Social planners Rittel and Webber (1973) distinguish between social problems and issues that are either "tame" or "wicked," ultimately defining ten inherent characteristics of the latter. To summarize simply, a wicked problem defies pragmatic or technical solutions because it is complex (i.e., it is an interrelated set of problems) and the solution is unclear (Head & Alford, 2015). In contrast, tame problems fit

S. Stone (✉)
School of Social Welfare, University of California at Berkeley, Berkeley, CA, USA
e-mail: sistone@berkeley.edu

© Springer Nature Switzerland AG 2019
C. C. Panlilio (ed.), *Trauma-Informed Schools*, Child Maltreatment Solutions
Network, https://doi.org/10.1007/978-3-030-12811-1_5

tight definitions, and, as a result, solutions (especially those that are technical in nature) can be identified and worked toward. Wicked problems receive a great deal of consideration in political science, planning, and public governance and management literatures, including consideration of the factors that shape them. Aside from the complexity of the problem itself, Head and Alford (2015) note that wicked problems correspond with conditions that include multiple stakeholders and multiple institutions ("diversity") and resource and knowledge uncertainty. Although wicked problems were initially framed as largely intractable, recent scholarship suggests possible ways to effectively address them (Head & Alford, 2015; Kolko, 2012).

## 5.3   Maltreatment as a Wicked Problem

Taking inspiration from this prior scholarship, this chapter argues that maltreatment is a wicked problem, highlighting its complexity, its stakeholder and institutional diversity, and its sources of resource and knowledge uncertainties.

### 5.3.1   Maltreatment as a Complex Problem

Prior research, including chapters in this volume, highlights the complexity of maltreatment as a social problem. Its scope is widespread (Stoltenborgh, Bakermans-Kranenburg, Alink, & van IJzendoorn, 2015) on national and global levels. In the United States, for example, maltreated children are often formally identified through state-level child abuse reporting systems. The most recent estimates suggest that, of four million referrals each year, nearly 60% are flagged for further investigation. These reports ultimately yield a child victimization rate of 9.2 per 1000. Children under the age of 1 represent the modal victim (24.2 per 1000 children in the population of the same age). Estimates of victimization rates among school-aged children range from 10.5 among 5- and 6-year-olds to 3.5 among 17-year-olds. Child victims are most likely to suffer from neglect (75%), followed by physical abuse (17.2) and sexual abuse (8.4). African-American children experience the highest rate of victimization at 14.5 per 1000 children.

As will be further elaborated below, formal state-level child welfare systems are a key institution charged to both identify and serve maltreated children and their families. Children and adolescents become involved in the child welfare system when reports of maltreatment are investigated (involving approximately 3.4 million children). Of these, 20% are ultimately identified as victims. While both victims and non-victims receive at least some post-response services from child welfare agencies, only a small share of victims (20%) ultimately receive foster care services. Among those placed in foster care, approximately half live in foster homes, one fourth with kin, and the remaining fourth in group care or other settings. Children under age 1 and over age 11 are most likely to be placed. The median length of stay by state ranges from 5 to 24 months. Half of foster youth experience at least one placement change, and 30% have three or more placement changes. Although most children and adolescents (60%) are reunified with their families, 20% are adopted. About 20% of youth will reenter the system within 2 years of their exit.

Further illustrating the complexity of maltreatment as a problem, there is general consensus that it is multiply determined by child, parent and family, social, and environmental factors (e.g., Belsky, 1993; Cicchetti & Toth, 2015) and, thus, best understood through a development-ecological-transactional framework (e.g., Cicchetti & Valentino, 2006). There is also growing consensus that child maltreatment is rooted in structural conditions. On the one hand, rates of county-level inequality relate to county-level maltreatment rates, controlling for child poverty rates (Eckenrode, Smith, McCarthy, & Dineen, 2014). An elevated risk of preventable mortality among African-American children is plausibly interpreted through a structural lens (Putnam-Hornstein, 2012). From the vantage point of child welfare system involvement and service provision, vexing racial disproportionalities and disparities emerge across key decision-making points in the system, many of which are poorly understood (Boyd, 2014; Bywaters et al., 2015; Putnam-Hornstein, Needell, King, & Johnson-Motoyama, 2013; Wulczyn, Gibbons, Snowden, & Lery, 2013).

Maltreatment is robustly linked with short- and long-term sequelae across educational, mental health, physical health, and other functional domains (Cicchetti, 2013; Font & Berger, 2015; Gilbert et al., 2009). Of particular relevance to the aims of this volume, experiences of child maltreatment and, relatedly, placement in foster care correspond to a variety of academic problems (for reviews, see Romano, Babchishin, Marquis, & Fréchette, 2015; Scherr, 2007; Stone, 2007). Notably, the root cause driving these relationships is challenging to ascertain, as both maltreatment and educational outcomes are associated with poverty and other family and environmental risks. Additionally, over and above sociodemographic risk factors, maltreatment relates to early cognitive deficits, lower standardized reading and mathematics test scores and grades, higher absenteeism, and increased likelihood of grade repetition (Font & Berger, 2015; Stone, 2007). Observed associations between maltreatment, early behavioral problems, placement in special education, and drop-out are largely accounted for by sociodemographic risk factors. Finally, among early elementary-aged students, both cognitive and non-cognitive variables associated with school success, such as teacher ratings of learning behaviors and skills like flexibility, persistence, and problem-solving, are inversely associated with maltreatment (Fantuzzo, Perlman, & Dobbins, 2011).

When well-matched controls are employed, out-of-home placement is not associated with poorer reading or mathematics skills (Berger, Cancian, Han, Noyes, & Rios-Salas, 2015). On the other hand, a meta-analysis of 31 studies concluded that foster children may be centrally characterized by elevated risk for grade retention, special education involvement, and disciplinary referrals (Scherr, 2007). School mobility appears to be a challenge for this population (Pears, Kim, Buchanan, & Fisher, 2015).

Given that a defining characteristic of a wicked problem is its intractability, multiple efforts to both prevent and selectively intervene in maltreatment show promising, albeit inconclusive, results (MacMillan et al., 2009; Mikton & Butchart, 2009). In addition, persistent problems of system-level and intraorganizational collaboration to support maltreated children with or without child welfare involvement abound (e.g., Ferguson & Wolkow, 2012; Stone & Zibulsky, 2015).

## 5.3.2  Organizational and Institutional Complexity

Wicked problems are also nested within organizationally and institutionally complex conditions (Head & Alford, 2015). Thus, attributes of child-serving systems, with a particular focus on their potentially divergent aims, normative and political contexts, and resource constraints are crucial to consider. Although the child welfare system plays central roles in the identification of and response to maltreatment, maltreated children are also potentially identified through schools and the juvenile justice and mental health systems. It is crucial that patterns of system involvement over time represent a key unit of analysis, as children may enter and exit various systems in unique ways over time (Wulczyn, Smithgall, & Chen, 2009). Although the system dynamics have been extensively reviewed elsewhere (see Stone & Zibulsky, 2015), the next sections highlight key attributes and dynamics of the child welfare, juvenile justice, and mental health systems, particularly as they broadly overlap with the experiences of various subgroups of maltreated children and the education system.

### 5.3.2.1  Child Welfare

As noted above, children and adolescents become involved in the child welfare system when reports of maltreatment are formally investigated. Scholars, however, question whether the term "child welfare system" best describes the character of this institution (Berrick, 2015; Wulczyn et al., 2013). Federal law mandates that child protection agencies exist and adhere to a broad set of requirements and goals, yet these agencies are administered at state and local levels, resulting in wide variation in state and local child welfare policies, responses, services, practices, and outcomes. At the front end of the system, referred children are assessed in terms of their risk of harm. A core systems goal is to ensure that children remain in their own homes, which necessitates balancing parental rights against risk of child harm. Once youth are removed, the goal is permanency. The Adoption and Safe Families Act (ASFA) of 1997 emphasizes strict time limits (12–18 months) on decisions to return children home or arrange for alternative plans (e.g., adoption).

Of note, recent legislation, the Fostering Connections to Success and Increasing Adoptions Act of 2008, underscores the importance of creating meaningful service-related connections between family or adoptive parents and older youth in the system. This act also emphasizes educational stability and opportunity, stating that child welfare agencies must create a plan for providing educational stability for foster children. If it is in the child's best interest, placement decisions must consider proximity to the child's original school; otherwise, case plans must ensure immediate and appropriate enrollment in a new school and ensure transfer of the student's educational records. The act also increased the amount of federal funding that can be used to cover education-related transportation.

Both scholars and legal advocates provide important critiques of the child welfare system, its scope, and goals. Berrick (2015) characterizes the system as one that prioritizes risk over need (i.e., formally identifying and serving only those at greatest risk of harm) and that is largely reactive in its approach to service provision. Moreover, the institutional character reflects fundamental and difficult to resolve tensions between optimizing child developmental outcomes through rich sets of services and family supports and, on the other hand, protecting family privacy from potentially overreaching state involvement (Berrick, 2015).

With respect to overlaps with the educational system, legal scholars note the weakness of accountability mechanisms in extant statutes to ensure focus on education outcomes and encourage meaningful collaboration between schools and child welfare agencies (Hahnel & Van Zile, 2012). Hahnel and Van Zile (2012) identify several constraints to productive collaboration on behalf of foster children. One is the school mobility of foster children; another is that the Family Educational Rights and Privacy Act (FERPA) only recently clarified provisions for information sharing between education and child welfare systems. The ease of record sharing, however, is often complicated by child welfare or school personnel knowledge about what aspects of the educational record should be shared, as well as the accessibility of various aspects of student academic records. Some research suggests that educational issues are often a low priority among child welfare workers, given their high caseloads and other crucial case-related demands such as placement availability (Zetlin & Weinberg, 2004).

There is also long-standing concern that foster youth, due to their caregiving arrangements, lack access to robust and consistent educational advocates. Unclear guardianship roles and responsibilities may contribute to delays in enrollment, as well discontinuities in educational programming for those students receiving or in need of special education services. Such issues appear to be pronounced for foster youth placed in residential care (Ayasse, Donahue, & Berrick, 2008).

### 5.3.2.2 Juvenile Justice

Crucially, youth who become involved in the juvenile justice system do overlap with those involved in the child welfare system. Experiencing maltreatment increases subsequent risk for delinquency and arrest (Bender, 2010), and sociodemographic risk factors for child welfare and juvenile justice involvement overlap (Sander, 2010). An emerging body of research considers so-called crossover youth, defined as those who have a history of maltreatment and have been identified by the juvenile justice system. This group of youth can be further delineated by the nature and timing of their identification with the child welfare and juvenile justice systems (Herz, Ryan, & Bilchik, 2010) and appear to have unique mental health and academic difficulties.

Scholars highlight three sets of system-level factors thought to contribute to the academic difficulties of incarcerated youth or to increase the risk of juvenile justice system involvement (Boundy & Karger, 2011). First, available evidence suggests limitations in both the quantity and quality of correctional education programs. A recent meta-analysis, for example, finds limited available academic interventions and reveals the difficulty of implementing such interventions (Sander, Patall, Amoscato, Fisher, & Funk, 2012). Second, youth transitioning into and out of the juvenile justice system encounter discontinuities in their academic trajectories. Discharge from the juvenile justice system operates as a critical transition point: estimates suggest that, post-discharge, fewer than half of youth transition back to school (Vacca, 2008). Moreover, post-discharge school performance, enrollment, and attendance are not systematically monitored (Boundy & Karger, 2011). Finally, school characteristics, policies, and practices—particularly school-level truancy rates, disciplinary policies, lax response to mental health needs, relational- and engagement-related attributes of school climate, and approaches to remediation of academic skills deficits—may induce risk for juvenile justice system involvement (Boundy & Karger, 2011; Sander, 2010).

Juvenile justice system normative and political dynamics show parallels to those of the child welfare system. Much like the child welfare system, the academic progress of affected children is not a central focus of this system (Wallace, 2012). The historical evolution of the system, moreover, reveals tensions centered on how to frame the problem of delinquency (individual versus ecological orientation), the relative benefits and effectiveness of diversion programs, and whether system goals should be oriented toward rehabilitation or punishment (Abrams, 2013).

### 5.3.2.3   Children's Mental Health

Recent meta-analytic and systematic reviews provide convincing evidence of a causal relationship between various forms of maltreatment and subsequent mental health difficulty (Edwards, Holden, Felitti, & Anda, 2003; Norman et al., 2012; Oswald, Heil, & Goldbeck, 2010). Echoing general themes discussed above pertaining to other child-serving systems of care, scholars document persistent difficulties in creating, sustaining, and authentically implementing mental health systems of care for children (Atkins & Frazier, 2011; Duchnowski & Kutash, 2007). In addition, there is persistent evidence that there is an unmet need for mental healthcare among children and that a complex set of both need and non-need factors such as sociodemographics shape access and utilization patterns (Jensen et al., 2011). A key and enduring challenge is the poor uptake of evidence-based intervention approaches (Weisz, Ugueto, Cheron, & Herren, 2013).

Crucially, schools are seen as a potentially important source of mental health service delivery, given that a substantial majority of schools (greater than 80%) provide some mental health services (Atkins & Lakind, 2013). Despite their potential as a service delivery site, Atkins and his colleagues contend that schools' roles in mental health service delivery are not adequately conceptualized, supported, or resourced (Atkins, Hoagwood, Kutash, & Seidman, 2010; Atkins & Lakind, 2013).

The preceding sections, which selectively examine attributes and dynamics of the child welfare, juvenile justice, and mental health systems, illustrate the institutional and organizational complexity relevant to children who have experienced maltreatment. Taken together, these sections suggest that children who have experienced maltreatment may (or, in some cases, may not) have unique sets of involvement with the child welfare, juvenile justice, and mental health systems. Given that maltreatment often co-occurs with academic, behavioral, and mental health difficulties, allied child-serving systems, due to unique and historically situated foci, typically do not orient toward education systems and have not typically centered the academic needs of this subgroup of children. Importantly, however, school practices—whether through routine practices or service delivery mechanisms—play crucial roles. Problems of collaborative and coordinated practices related to maltreated children are consistently referenced across these literatures.

### 5.3.2.4 Schools

It is notable that scholarship on child-serving systems of care typically does not consider the unique institutional and organizational dynamics associated with the educational system in general or schools in particular (Atkins & Lakind, 2013; Stone & Moragne, 2016). Historians of education persuasively demonstrate how the goals of schooling reflect dominant, albeit contested, values and how schools are often assigned to respond to vexing social issues (Cuban, 2013; Deschenes, Cuban, & Tyack, 2001). In the former case, for example, recurring cycles of emphasis on achievement of standards versus more individualized whole-child approaches reflect larger tensions in societal values (Cuban, 2012).

Given such forces, schools and districts maintain fairly stable organizational structures that are often taken for granted: age-graded classrooms, teacher-centered pedagogical practices, typical sequences of curricula, and centralized bureaucratic structures, for example (Deschenes et al., 2001). Schools, and particularly classroom practices, are difficult to reform (Cuban, 2013).

Schools, both currently and historically, function as key sites of health and psychosocial service delivery (Tyack, 1992). Yet, funding for school-based health, mental health, and social service delivery has historically been and currently is inconsistent and uneven (Tyack, 1992). Extant psychosocial interventions often do not have instructional levers strong enough to push meaningful academic growth (Atkins & Lakind, 2013). These limitations must be deeply considered, given the academic difficulties documented among maltreated subgroups of children and those placed in out-of-home care (see Stone, 2007).

Given that schools are difficult to reform, key bodies of educational research point directly to elements of well-functioning school environments. Stone and Moragne (2016) provide a summary of school effectiveness research (see also Bryk, 2010). This line of research identifies potentially malleable school conditional attributes that are linked to student engagement and achievement under specific conditions. These conditions include (a) relational trust across the school community; (b) strong principal leadership; (c) meaningful parent-school-community ties; (d) a student-centered instructional climate, characterized by both rigor and support; and (e) coherent instructional programming linked to teacher professional development and a culture of innovation among staff members. Such conditions echo processes associated with trauma-sensitive school environments and successful implementations of evidence-based interventions.

While school effectiveness research considers the school organizational conditions that increase potential for student growth, Weinstein and Worrell (2016) extend the discussion to effective arrangements of school-based student supports. Their approach and others, centered in urban school reform, critique the usual practices in schools to add programs to respond to specific student support needs (see also Atkins & Lakind, 2013). Instead, they advocate core, so-called "SMART" principles of school support services. These principles (a) include school-wide delivery strategies that are student- and family-strength focused and are designed to reduce stigma; (b) target multiple domains of student functioning, designed to be responsive to the multicultural backgrounds of students and families; (c) are aligned with and flexibly adapted to instructional and other core school activities; (d) are relationally oriented; and (e) reflect public health approaches to school-based service delivery and are both timely and tiered, attending to cascades of services ranging from prevention to intervention efforts. Of note, Weinstein and Worrell (2016) document the extensive in-school collaborative efforts needed to enact such principles.

## 5.4 Responding to Wicked Problems

The prior sections built an argument that maltreatment ought to be viewed as a wicked problem given its underlying complexity as well as the diverse nature of the wider institutional and organizational field in which it is embedded. Where does such a framing ultimately lead? On the one hand, Head and Alford (2015) observe that "[a]t first sight, grappling with wicked problems might seem like taking up lost causes" (p. 712). On the other hand, there is a growing body of scholarship that suggests considerations in approaching wicked problems.

### 5.4.1  Authoritative and Collaborative Approaches

Roberts (2000), for example, centers on power relations as one way of approaching wicked problems. In the simplest terms, she suggests that solutions hinge on authoritative versus collaborative approaches which, applied to the problem of maltreatment, suggests that vesting authority within one stakeholder may be a route to resolution. For example, as noted above, Berrick (2015) notes the circumscribed roles the US child welfare system assumes by targeting the highest risk families for services and intervention. In contrast, Finland's promotion of child and family well-being is more centrally administered. Collaborative approaches represent another option. A collaborative approach might, for example, involve high-level stakeholders across education and other systems of care to jointly craft a strategic plan specifically focused on addressing academic issues among maltreated children. An example of such an approach is exemplified by the Crossover Youth Practice Model that seeks to reduce these youths' recidivism in the juvenile justice system (Haight, Bidwell, Marshall, & Khatiwoda, 2014).

### 5.4.2  Process Approaches

Head and Alford (2015) assert that wicked problems themselves are heterogeneous and suggest that attention be paid to what underlying wicked forces drive the problem. For example, some unique combination of knowledge gaps, stakeholder value differences, and problems of collaboration form a given wicked problem. From this perspective, an important set of steps involves analyzing these underlying issues within a collaborative framework. In this case, multiple stakeholder perspectives are necessary for an in-depth analysis of the particular nature of the wicked problem. Central to these problem-solving processes are innovative forms of collaborative leadership. Importantly, Head and Alford (2015) assert that collaborative forms of leadership are not the norm in traditional policy and practice environments. In the context of child maltreatment, a collaborative leadership approach would acknowledge and tackle the routine forms of centralized leadership across schools and other child-serving systems of care that undergird long-standing and well-documented problems in collaboration and coordination across multiple levels of these systems.

### 5.4.3  Design Thinking Approaches

Kolko (2012) adds further nuance to the preceding approaches. Writing from the perspective of promoting innovation, Kolko (2012) argues for interdisciplinary problem-solving approaches that appreciate the complexity of the underlying problem to be solved and refrain from "quick fixes." For example, typical responses to academic difficulties among maltreated children come in the form of particular programs. Kolko (2012), however, advocates for persistent and rigorous iterations of approaches that directly involve those directly affected. Indeed, maltreated children and their caregivers are rarely involved in problem-solving processes aimed at improvements in service or policy. This is especially of concern given the formidable demands on families involved in the child welfare system (Barth, 2015).

## 5.5 Concluding Comments

This chapter applied the concept of a "wicked problem" to child maltreatment. The complexities of child maltreatment, including its multiple and multilevel determinants and consequences, were selectively reviewed. In addition, the diversity of the institutional and organizational fields in which child maltreatment is embedded was described. A key point was that the problem of maltreatment cuts across multiple child-serving systems, including child welfare, juvenile justice, and mental health as well as education. Crucially, educational performance is not a shared goal across these systems, and there is evidence for long-standing and embedded problems of coordination and collaboration.

While it does not offer a concrete strategy for resolution, this chapter suggests that the problem of maltreatment is unlikely to be "solved" by a specific set of programs or policies. Instead, more fruitful steps forward would emphasize a common framing of maltreatment as a wicked problem; renewed efforts to distill the specific aspects of wickedness related to maltreatment in the areas of complexity, diversity, and uncertainty (Head & Alford, 2015); and heightened attention, at the very least, to well-documented and multilevel problems of coordination and collaboration related to maltreated children. Such steps would likely be enhanced if they directly involved maltreated children and their caregivers.

## References

Abrams, L. S. (2013). Juvenile justice at a crossroads: Science, evidence, and twenty-first century reform. *Social Service Review, 87*, 725–752.

Atkins, M., Hoagwood, K., Kutash, K., & Seidman, E. (2010). Towards the integration of education and mental health in schools. *Administration and Policy in Mental Health and Mental Health Services Research, 37*, 40–47.

Atkins, M. S., & Frazier, S. L. (2011). Expanding the toolkit or changing the paradigm: Are we ready for a public health approach to mental health? *Perspectives on Psychological Science, 6*(5), 483–487.

Atkins, M. S., & Lakind, D. (2013). Usual care for clinicians, unusual care for their clients: Rearranging priorities for children's mental health services. *Administration and Policy in Mental Health and Mental Health Services Research, 40*, 48–51.

Ayasse, R. H., Donahue, J., & Berrick, J. D. (2008). The school enrollment process for group home youth. *Journal of Public Child Welfare, 1*, 95–113.

Barth, R. P. (2015). Commentary on the report of the APSAC Task Force on evidence-based service planning guidelines for child welfare. *Child Maltreatment, 20*, 17–19.

Belsky, J. (1993). Etiology of child maltreatment: A developmental-ecological analysis. *Psychological Bulletin, 114*, 413–434.

Bender, K. (2010). Why do some maltreated youth become juvenile offenders?: A call for further investigation and adaptation of youth services. *Children and Youth Services Review, 32*, 466–473.

Berger, L. M., Cancian, M., Han, E., Noyes, J., & Rios-Salas, V. (2015). Children's academic achievement and foster care. *Pediatrics, 135*, 109–116.

Berrick, J. D. (2015). Protecting children from maltreatment in the United States. *Arbor, 197*, 1–10. https://doi.org/10.3989/arbor.2015.771n1005

Boundy, K. B., & Karger, J. (2011). The right to a quality education for children and youth in the juvenile justice system. In F. T. Sherman & F. H. Jacobs (Eds.), *Juvenile justice: Advancing research, policy, and practice* (pp. 129–201). Hoboken, NJ: Wiley.

Boyd, R. (2014). African American disproportionality and disparity in child welfare: Toward a comprehensive conceptual framework. *Children and Youth Services Review, 37*, 15–27.

Bryk, A. S. (2010). Organizing schools for improvement. *Phi Delta Kappan, 91*, 23–30.

Bywaters, P., Brady, G., Sparks, T., Bos, E., Bunting, L., Daniel, B., … Scourfield, J. (2015). Exploring inequities in child welfare and child protection services: Explaining the 'inverse intervention law. *Children and Youth Services Review, 57*, 98–105.

Cicchetti, D. (2013). Annual research review: Resilient functioning in maltreated children: Past, present, and future perspectives. *Journal of Child Psychology and Psychiatry, and Allied Disciplines, 54*, 402–422. https://doi.org/10.1111/j.1469-7610.2012.02608.x

Cicchetti, D., & Toth, S. L. (2015). Multilevel developmental perspectives on child maltreatment. *Development and Psychopathology, 27*, 1385–1386.

Cicchetti, D., & Valentino, K. (2006). An ecological-transactional perspective on child maltreatment: Failure of the average expectable environment and its influence on child development. In D. Cicchetti & D. Cohen (Eds.), *Developmental Psychopathology* (2nd ed., pp. 129–201). New York, NY: Wiley.

Cuban, L. (2012). Standards vs. customization: Finding the balance. *Educational Leadership, 69*, 10–15.

Cuban, L. (2013). Why so many structural changes in schools and so little reform in teaching practice? *Journal of Educational Administration, 51*, 109–125.

Deschenes, S., Cuban, L., & Tyack, D. (2001). Mismatch: Historical perspectives on schools and students who don't fit them. *Teachers College Record, 103*, 525–547.

Duchnowski, A. J., & Kutash, K. (2007). *Family-driven care*. Tampa, FL: University of South Florida.

Eckenrode, J., Smith, E. G., McCarthy, M. E., & Dineen, M. (2014). Income inequality and child maltreatment in the United States. *Pediatrics, 133*, 454–461.

Edwards, V. J., Holden, G. W., Felitti, V. J., & Anda, R. F. (2003). Relationship between multiple forms of childhood maltreatment and adult mental health in community respondents: Results from the adverse childhood experiences study. *American Journal of Psychiatry, 160*, 1453–1460.

Fantuzzo, J. W., Perlman, S. M., & Dobbins, E. K. (2011). Types and timing of child maltreatment and early school success: A population-based investigation. *Children and Youth Services Review, 33*, 1404–1411.

Ferguson, H. B., & Wolkow, K. (2012). Educating children and youth in care: A review of barriers to school progress and strategies for change. *Children and Youth Services Review, 34*, 1143–1149.

Font, S. A., & Berger, L. M. (2015). Child maltreatment and children's developmental trajectories in early- to middle-childhood. *Child Development, 86*, 536–556. https://doi.org/10.1111/cdev.12322

Gilbert, R., Widom, C. S., Browne, K., Fergusson, D., Webb, E., & Janson, S. (2009). Burden and consequences of child maltreatment in high-income countries. *Lancet, 373*, 68–81.

Hahnel, J., & Van Zile, C. (2012). The other achievement gap: Court-dependent youth and educational advocacy. *Journal of Law & Education. 41*, 435–481.

Haight, W. L., Bidwell, L. N., Marshall, J. M., & Khatiwoda, P. (2014). Implementing the Crossover Youth Practice Model in diverse contexts: Child welfare and juvenile justice professionals' experiences of multisystem collaborations. *Children and Youth Services Review, 39*, 91–100.

Head, B. W., & Alford, J. (2015). Wicked problems: Implications for public policy and management. *Administration & Society, 47*, 711–739.

Herz, D. C., Ryan, J. P., & Bilchik, S. (2010). Challenges facing crossover youth: An examination of juvenile-justice decision making and recidivism. *Family Court Review, 48*, 305–321.

Jensen, P. S., Goldman, E., Offord, D., Costello, E. J., Friedman, R., Huff, B., ... Conger, R. (2011). Overlooked and underserved: "Action signs" for identifying children with unmet mental health needs. *Pediatrics, 128*, 970–979.

Kolko, J. (2012). *Wicked problems: Problems worth solving*. Austin, TX: Austin Center for Design.

MacMillan, H. L., Wathen, C. N., Barlow, J., Fergusson, D. M., Leventhal, J. M., & Taussig, H. N. (2009). Interventions to prevent child maltreatment and associated impairment. *The Lancet, 373*, 250–266.

Mikton, C., & Butchart, A. (2009). Child maltreatment prevention: A systematic review of reviews. *Bulletin of the World Health Organization, 87*, 353–361.

Norman, R. E., Byambaa, M., De, R., Butchart, A., Scott, J., & Vos, T. (2012). The long-term health consequences of child physical abuse, emotional abuse, and neglect: A systematic review and meta-analysis. *PLoS Medicine, 9*, e1001349. https://doi.org/10.1371/journal.pmed.1001349

Oswald, S. H., Heil, K., & Goldbeck, L. (2010). History of maltreatment and mental health problems in foster children: A review of the literature. *Journal of Pediatric Psychology, 35*, 462–472.

Pears, K. C., Kim, H. K., Buchanan, R., & Fisher, P. A. (2015). Adverse consequences of school mobility for children in foster care: A prospective longitudinal study. *Child Development, 86*, 1210–1226.

Putnam-Hornstein, E. (2012). Preventable injury deaths: A population-based proxy of child maltreatment risk in California. *Public Health Reports, 127*, 163–172.

Putnam-Hornstein, E., Needell, B., King, B., & Johnson-Motoyama, M. (2013). Racial and ethnic disparities: A population-based examination of risk factors for involvement with child protective services. *Child Abuse & Neglect, 37*, 33–46.

Rittel, H. W., & Webber, M. M. (1973). Planning problems are wicked. *Polity, 4*, 155–169.

Roberts, N. (2000). Wicked problems and network approaches to resolution. *International Public Management Review, 1*, 1–19.

Romano, E., Babchishin, L., Marquis, R., & Fréchette, S. (2015). Childhood maltreatment and educational outcomes. *Trauma, Violence, & Abuse, 16*, 418–437.

Sander, J. B. (2010). School psychology, juvenile justice, and the school to prison pipeline. *NASP Communiqué, 39*, 4–6.

Sander, J. B., Patall, E. A., Amoscato, L. A., Fisher, A. L., & Funk, C. (2012). A meta-analysis of the effect of juvenile delinquency interventions on academic outcomes. *Children and Youth Services Review, 34*, 1695–1708.

Scherr, T. G. (2007). Educational experiences of children in foster care meta-analyses of special education, retention and discipline rates. *School Psychology International, 28*, 419–436.

Stoltenborgh, M., Bakermans-Kranenburg, M. J., Alink, L. R., & van IJzendoorn, M. H. (2015). The prevalence of child maltreatment across the globe: Review of a series of meta-analyses. *Child Abuse Review, 24*, 37–50.

Stone, S. (2007). Child maltreatment, out-of-home placement and academic vulnerability: A fifteen-year review of evidence and future directions. *Children and Youth Services Review, 29*, 139–161.

Stone, S., & Moragne, K. (2016). The changing contexts of school social work practice. In L. Villareal Sosa, T. Cox, & M. Alvarez (Eds.), *School social work: National perspectives on practice in schools* (pp. 69–82). New York, NY: Oxford University Press.

Stone, S., & Zibulsky, J. (2015). Maltreatment, academic difficulty, and systems-involved youth: Current evidence and opportunities. *Psychology in the Schools, 52*(1), 22–39.

Tyack, D. (1992). Health and social services in public schools: Historical perspectives. *The Future of Children, 2*(1), 19–31.

Vacca, J. S. (2008). Crime can be prevented if schools teach juvenile offenders to read. *Children and Youth Services Review, 30,* 1055–1062.

Wallace, P. (2012). Juvenile justice and education: Identifying leverage points and recommending reform for re-entry in Washington, DC. *Georgetown Journal on Poverty Law and Policy, 19,* 159–179.

Weinstein, R. S., & Worrell, F. C. (2016). *Achieving college dreams: How a university-charter district partnership created an early college high school.* New York, NY: Oxford University Press.

Weisz, J. R., Ugueto, A. M., Cheron, D. M., & Herren, J. (2013). Evidence-based youth psychotherapy in the mental health ecosystem. *Journal of Clinical Child & Adolescent Psychology, 42,* 274–286.

Wulczyn, F., Gibbons, R., Snowden, L., & Lery, B. (2013). Poverty, social disadvantage, and the black/white placement gap. *Children and Youth Services Review, 35,* 65–74. https://doi.org/10.1016/j.childyouth.2012.10.005

Wulczyn, F., Smithgall, C., & Chen, L. (2009). Child well-being: The intersection of schools and child welfare. *Review of Research in Education, 33,* 35–62.

Zetlin, A. G., & Weinberg, L. A. (2004). Understanding the plight of foster youth and improving their educational opportunities. *Child Abuse & Neglect, 28,* 917–923.

# Chapter 6
# Responding to Childhood Trauma at the Macro- and Microsystem Levels: The Necessity for Trauma-Sensitive Pedagogy

Christy Tirrell-Corbin

## 6.1 Introduction

While many adults have an idyllic view of childhood, children around the world are regularly exposed to traumatic events that overwhelm their capacity to cope (Atwoli, Stein, Koenen, & McLaughlin, 2015; National Child Traumatic Stress Network, 2003). As a result, children experience traumatic stress that manifests itself in myriad ways, some of which are devastating for their teachers who are almost universally unprepared to respond to and cope with resulting behaviors. The following anecdotes reflect actual examples:

*A 4-year-old child brought her cat into her preschool classroom for Show 'n Tell. While waiting for her turn, the child strangled her cat to death.*
*A third-grade child burst into tears when asked to write about a challenge he has overcome; the assignment reminded him of his cousin's murder the summer before.*

The purpose of this paper is to provide a foundation for macro- and microsystem (Bronfenbrenner, 1981; Bronfenbrenner & Morris, 2006) responses to childhood trauma, with a particular emphasis on the early childhood years (birth through age 8). The types, prevalence, and consequences of trauma will be presented, as will evidence regarding mandated teacher reporting and teachers' secondary trauma resulting from working in settings with high rates of adversity. The issue of trauma will also be explored through recent macro- and microsystem initiatives in the United States. Finally, examples of trauma-sensitive pedagogy, at the pre-ser-

C. Tirrell-Corbin (✉)
Center for Early Childhood Education and Intervention, Department of Human Development and Quantitative Methodology, University of Maryland, College Park, MD, USA
e-mail: ctc@umd.edu

© Springer Nature Switzerland AG 2019                                                     93
C. C. Panlilio (ed.), *Trauma-Informed Schools*, Child Maltreatment Solutions Network, https://doi.org/10.1007/978-3-030-12811-1_6

vice and in-service level, will be offered as a strategy for supporting a positive trajectory for children who are otherwise at risk when it comes to their development and learning.

## 6.2 Defining Childhood Trauma

The Florida State University Center for Prevention and Early Intervention Policy (2014) defines trauma as "an event that is unpredictable, produces feelings of helplessness, and overwhelms one's capacity to cope." These traumatic events can either be acute, such as the sudden loss of a loved one, school violence, or natural disasters, or chronic (e.g., neighborhood violence, homelessness, poverty, maternal depression, intimate partner violence, or complex trauma) (Jones Harden, 2015; National Scientific Council on the Developing Child, 2005/2014). When children are exposed to multiple or prolonged traumatic events, often involving chronic child maltreatment, the resulting complex trauma begins early in life and occurs with their primary caregivers, resulting in toxic stress. Young children "are often exposed to chronic and complex trauma because one traumatic experience may relate to another (e.g., the co-occurrence of intimate partner violence and child abuse)" (Jones Harden, 2015, p. 2). The US Department of Health and Human Services (2016) estimates that there were 702,000 child victims of maltreatment in 2014. Rates of victimization were highest for infants under 1 (24.4 per 1000 children), followed by children between the ages of 1 and 5 (11.4 per 1000 children), and then children between 6 and 10 (9.0 per 1000).

Such early experiences often negatively impact brain structures and functioning, as well as socioemotional functioning that have negative cascading effects on their learning processes; "In extreme cases, such as cases of severe, chronic abuse (especially during early, sensitive periods of brain development), the regions of the brain involved in fear, anxiety and impulsive responses may overproduce neural connections while those regions dedicated to reasoning, planning, and behavioral control may produce fewer neural connections" (National Scientific Council on the Developing Child, 2005/2014, p. 2). Consequently, children who display fear, anxiety, and impulsive responses are more likely to experience school (including preschool) expulsions or suspension (National Scientific Council on the Developing Child, 2005/2014), especially if they are of color and notably African American (Gilliam, Maupin, Reyes, Accavitti, & Shic, 2016). Moreover children with disabilities or developmental delays are more likely to experience abuse and neglect; at the same time, children who are abused and neglected are more likely to be identified as having a disability or developmental delay (Maryland State Department of Education, 2015). As a case in point, children of color in the state of Maryland are disproportionally represented both in special education and removal from school through suspension or expulsion (Maryland State Department of Education, 2016).

## 6.3   Childhood Trauma and Teacher Reporting

Teachers are the second largest reporting source (17.7%) of child maltreatment in the United States (U.S. Department of Health and Human Services, 2016), which is not surprising given their daily contact with children (Alisic, 2012; Brubacher, Powell, Snow, Skouteris, & Manger, 2016; Kenny, 2004; Walkley & Cox, 2013). Nonetheless, evidence suggests that teachers have limited knowledge of the signs and symptoms of child maltreatment in spite of the mandatory child abuse and reporting laws that exist across the country (Kenny, 2004; Walter, Gouze, & Lim, 2006). One potential reason for that limited knowledge is that teacher education programs leave professional development regarding reporting laws to local schools and school systems instead of incorporating that content into their teacher education curricula (Farrell & Walsh, 2010; Goldman & Grimbeek, 2014). Furthermore, teachers are often reluctant to report suspected abuse and neglect due to limited understanding of maltreatment (Walter et al., 2006), state laws and definitions of reporting (Flaherty et al., 2006), and the incorrect belief that their role is to investigate suspected abuse or neglect (Kenny, 2004). As a result, evidence suggests that teachers typically rely on school psychologists to address trauma-related issues faced by their students (Alisic, 2012; Viezel & Davis, 2014) rather than address it by themselves or in collaboration with the school psychologist. In response to the inconsistent reporting and responses to maltreatment, Kenny (2004) recommended standardized training in child maltreatment for all teachers and Brubacher et al. (2016) identified interviewing skills as important for teachers given their daily interactions with children throughout the school year.

## 6.4   Consequences of Childhood Trauma

Trauma often results in social, emotional, and academic challenges in the context of the classroom due to a lack of adult support, decreased resilience, and changes in brain structure (Carrion, Weems, & Reiss, 2007; Dykman et al., 1997; Evans, Davies, & DiLillo, 2008; Kim & Cicchetti, 2010; Shields & Cicchetti, 2001). As a result of early traumatic experiences, children often fall behind non-maltreated and non-traumatized children in measures of educational achievement. Rouse and Fantuzzo (2009) found that childhood maltreatment, even after controlling for poverty, maternal education, and homelessness, was the strongest predictor of poor math and reading achievement as early as third grade. Teachers' lack of preparedness to respond to such behaviors may result in an overreliance on discipline practices (including suspension and expulsion) that do not consider the underlying reason for children's behaviors (Gilliam et al., 2016). It is therefore imperative that school administrators carefully examine the disparate impact of discipline practices on different student populations, particularly those with traumatic histories (Morgan, Salomon, Plotkin, & Cohen, 2014). Examining disciplinary policies and data is especially necessary for children with a history of traumatic events given the important role of teachers as non-familial adults who may function as secondary attachment figures for this vulnerable group of students (Lynch & Cicchetti, 1992).

Taken together, the high prevalence of early traumatic experience in early childhood and its negative impact on educational, emotional, and behavioral outcomes at the end of the early childhood period highlight the need for education-focused prevention and intervention efforts during this sensitive period of development. The classroom, in particular, becomes an important microsystem wherein teachers must be supported in order to promote a positive trajectory in these at-risk students' development and learning. In fact, evidence suggests that opportunities for play, socialization, and interactions with nurturing caregivers and other adults (e.g., teachers) can help to mediate the consequences of toxic stress (National Scientific Council on the Developing Child, 2005/2014). Furthermore, teachers can offer stable, safe spaces for children, places away from neighborhood and domestic violence where children feel valued and respected (Cole, Eisner, Gregory, & Ristuccia, 2013). Teachers are also in a position to teach children self-regulation strategies and mindfulness, which reduce stress and therefore promote learning. Lastly, teachers have the ability to provide children with opportunities for success that might otherwise be rare.

## 6.5 Secondary Trauma

Reporting suspected maltreatment and responding to other childhood traumas are typically daunting and emotional tasks for teachers. Alisic (2012) identified the challenges that teachers encountered in trying to balance the needs of children who had experienced trauma with those who had not. She also found that teachers struggle with the "emotional burden" (also known as secondary trauma) of working with children/students who had experienced trauma.

Similarly, Bride, Robinson, Yegidis, and Figley (2004) studied the consequences of secondary trauma in social workers, which led to the identification of 17 different responses to secondary trauma ranging from difficulty concentrating to feeling emotionally numb to having little interest in being around others. Not surprisingly, Jennings and Greenberg (2009) argued for the importance of teachers' socioemotional competence (SEC) in the classroom. If not attended to, frustration with student behaviors can cascade into teacher burnout. The burnout rate is exacerbated due to the challenges and stress associated with teaching children who have experienced—or are experiencing—trauma (VanBergeijk & Sarmiento, 2006).

Ingersoll and Merrill (2010) reported the hiring of approximately 200,000 new teachers each year in the United States, with approximately 10% leaving teaching in their first year and 45% leaving after 5 years. While there are many reasons that teachers leave the profession, the works of Jennings and Greenberg (2009) and VanBergeijk and Sarmiento (2006) suggest that burnout due to their lack of preparation to meet the needs of children in adverse circumstances contributes to the low retention rate.

## 6.6   Macrosystem Responses to Childhood Trauma

Although childhood trauma has been linked to unemployment, incarceration, and drug use, macrosystem responses have been scarce. In 2014, through the advocacy efforts of the Massachusetts Advocates for Children Trauma and Learning Policy Initiative (TLPI), Massachusetts passed the Safe and Supportive Schools Act V (Cole, 2014; Massachusetts Safe and Supportive Schools Commission, 2017). The Safe and Supportive Schools Act resulted in a statewide infrastructure focused on processes and tools necessary for schools to provide safe and supportive environments for learning. It is important to note that the focus on schools included all personnel—administrators, teachers, bus drivers, cafeteria staff, and so on—rather than individual teachers and classrooms, which is a central principle of TLPI's work (Cole et al., 2013).

Washington State has a trauma-informed instruction initiative that articulates pedagogical practices necessary to support children's emotion regulation and social emotional learning (Wolpow, Johnson, Hertel, & Kincaid, 2009). The State of Washington Office of Superintendent of Public Instruction (OSPI) now offers a social emotional learning (SEL) module, which was developed at the direction of the Washington State Legislature in 2015. The SEL module is offered as part of Washington's OSPI professional learning program (State of Washington Office of Superintendent of Public Instruction, 2018 March), allowing educators to complete the module for continuing education credits. SEL is comprised of five learning segments: introduction of SEL, embedding SEL school-wide, creating a professional culture based in SEL, integrating SEL into culturally responsive classrooms, and identifying and selecting evidence-based programs (State of Washington Office of Superintendent of Public Instruction, 2018 May).

While Massachusetts and Washington have trauma-sensitive initiatives, federal efforts in response to trauma were disparate and unorganized until the 2017 introduction of trauma-sensitive legislation in the US Congress. House Bill 1757, the Trauma-Informed Care for Children and Families Act, includes a focus on teacher preparation, teacher retention, trauma identification, discipline policies, and school climate. House Bill 1757 stalled in committee and never made it to a vote in the House of Representatives or the US Senate.

## 6.7   Microsystem Responses: Trauma-Sensitive Pedagogy

Although the knowledge base around childhood trauma has expanded significantly in recent decades, as evidenced by macrosystem responses in Massachusetts, Washington State, and Washington, D.C., most trauma-focused professional development efforts for educators have centered on mandated reporter training or a general onetime overview about trauma. Though important in providing the necessary tools for understanding, detection, and reporting, this strategy lacks the knowledge requisite to fully understand the developmental impact of early traumatic experiences on this vulnerable group of students. Furthermore, this approach ignores principles of both adult learning theory (Cox, 2015; Knowles, 1973) and improvement science (Bryk, Gomez, Grunow, & LeMahieu, 2015), which suggest that learning experiences must be grounded in active engagement, problem-centered learning, prior/current knowledge, and experiences in the classroom/school. Perhaps as importantly, these trainings lack guidance on how the developmental impact of trauma should be used to inform pedagogy and one's own self-care.

In a national needs assessment for a trauma-sensitive curriculum conducted by Tirrell-Corbin, Panlilio, and Ferrara (2018), over 700 respondents indicated that they lacked the knowledge and skills necessary to meet the emotional needs of their own students when the respondents first began their educational career. Moreover, 98% ($N = 941$) of respondents agreed or strongly agreed that there was a need for trauma-sensitive curricula and identified several key components, including the developmental effect of trauma, pedagogical strategies appropriate for children who have experienced trauma, self-care strategies for teachers, building relationships with community members, and advocating for trauma-sensitive schools.

## 6.8   Implications for Practice

The National Scientific Council on the Developing Child (2005/2014), the Trauma and Learning Policy Initiative (TLPI) from the Massachusetts Advocates for Children and Harvard Law School (Cole et al., 2013), and the recent position statement by the Division for Early Childhood (2016) of the Council for Exceptional Children have all articulated the need to further understand the impact of trauma on education. Specifically, the Division for Early Childhood (DEC) (2016) recommends that educators and educational researchers work toward prevention and intervention by identifying evidence-based practices that can be embedded within DEC-recommended practices. Consequently, it is essential that policymakers, researchers, and practitioners expand their focus on professional development opportunities related to childhood trauma at both the pre- and in-service levels.

As previously mentioned, the attrition rate in education is high with approximately 45% of US teachers leaving the classroom within 5 years (Ingersoll & Merrill, 2010). While there are numerous factors that influence a teacher's decision to stay in or leave education, evidence suggests that being unprepared to meet the needs of children with adverse experiences (Gilliam et al., 2016; Tirrell-Corbin et al., 2018) and secondary traumatic stress (Jennings & Greenberg, 2009; VanBergeijk & Sarmiento, 2006) are important considerations. Moreover, data also indicate that beginning teachers are much more likely to be hired into schools in high-poverty communities with high rates of teacher turnover (Gagnon & Mattingly, 2012). These findings alone are sufficient reasons to reconsider the way teachers are prepared and supported (e.g., in-service professional development, coaching, and teaming) in contemporary classrooms. However, the plethora of data on the consequences of childhood trauma makes the case even more compelling (Carrion et al., 2007; Dykman et al., 1997; Evans et al., 2008; Kim & Cicchetti, 2010; Shields & Cicchetti, 2001).

Given the prevalence of maltreatment in the early years (U.S. Department of Health and Human Services, 2017) and the interconnectedness between childhood trauma and special education referrals (Maryland State Department of Education, 2015), the remainder of this paper will focus on pre- and in-service trauma-sensitive pedagogy for early childhood and special education teachers, specialists, and administrators.

### 6.8.1   Trauma-Sensitive Pedagogy: A Pre-service Example

Teacher education programs are overseen by an array of regulatory bodies and agencies that include, but are not limited to, regulations and laws overseen by state departments of education; the national Council for the Accreditation of Educator Preparation (CAEP); and specialty professional associations such as the Council for Exceptional Children (CEC) and the National Association for the Education of Young Children (NAEYC), each of them with their own sets of standards and expectations.

Notably, the CEC (2012) and NAEYC (2010) have a strong focus on the whole child; their standards address child development, family relationships, advocacy, and developmental differences. Nonetheless, teacher education programs in early childhood and special education still vary in terms of focus on childhood trauma, and there is no standard from either the CEC or NAEYC that focuses on coping with secondary trauma.

Building on CAEP Standard 2: Clinical Partnerships and Practice, notably 2.1, which focuses on the co-construction of mutually beneficial P–12 school and community arrangements (Council for the Accreditation of Educator Preparation, 2013), an essential step in the design of trauma-sensitive teacher preparation programs is the collaborative development or redesign of teacher education programs with school system partners. Strategies for implementing this work include needs assessments, document review (especially syllabi), and focus groups with an array of stakeholders.

An example of the co-construction of a mutually beneficial teacher education is illustrated in the design of the Early Childhood/Early Childhood Special Education (EC/ECSE) at the University of Maryland (Klein, Tirrell-Corbin, & Lieber, in press). The EC/ECSE program is a 4-year baccalaureate degree program resulting in eligibility for state certification in both early childhood education (preschool through third grade) and early childhood special education (birth through third grade). CEC and NAEYC standards are fully integrated into every course and field experience, including the final, senior year internship where teacher candidates are required to meet both CEC and NAEYC sets of professional standards for a beginning teacher. EC/ECSE students choose a specialty track that focuses on birth through kindergarten or preschool through third grade, allowing them to develop knowledge and skills appropriate for the settings in which they intend to teach. The program replaced a 4-year baccalaureate degree program in ECE and a 5-year master's degree program in ECSE, which makes the EC/ECSE degree requirements particularly rigorous given that the same content has been condensed into a single 4-year program.

A first step in the design of the EC/ECSE program was the facilitation of a focus group comprised of various stakeholders from four partner schools within the county. Participants included teachers, instructional specialists, a principal, and the chief academic officer of a large district (over 125,000 students with a roughly 60% free and reduced meal rate). Course syllabi were sent to school-system personnel for review and feedback. After the curriculum was drafted, the stakeholder focus group was reconvened to review the design and provide final feedback. Only after all stakeholder feedback was considered and incorporated into the curriculum did the program faculty submit the degree program and courses to the university approval processes.

As a direct result of the focus group discussion, the EC/ECSE program was designed to include a strong focus on preparing teachers to respond to challenging, aggressive, and even violent behaviors. Teacher candidates take courses entitled Interventions for Children with Behavioral Challenges, which focuses on functional behavioral assessments such as data collection of on-task positive behaviors, and Interventions for Children with Social Communications. At the suggestion of the chief academic officer, the program includes opportunities for teacher candidates to be exposed to case management skills that are typically taught in schools of social work.

The EC/ECSE program includes several courses that address childhood trauma, child maltreatment, brain development, social emotional development, and education policy. A strengths-based perspective when working with children and families is the overarching focus. In response to the fact that new teaching positions are typically in urban environments (Gagnon & Mattingly, 2012), the program also has a strategic, intentional focus on placing teacher candidates in Title I (high poverty) childcare centers, early intervention programs, and public schools throughout their five semesters of placements.

Course and placement assignments include, but are not limited to, a reflective paper on one's family of origin, intended to give teacher candidates a greater understanding of themselves as a means of understanding and respecting others; reading and analysis of *Fire in the Ashes* (Kozol, 2012) in conjunction with news articles highlighting local examples of inequity and adversity; and a semester-long project that begins with a research paper on an adverse issue such as homelessness, child abuse and neglect, and parental divorce and concludes with writing a children's book on the topic so that candidates simultaneously increase their knowledge and are better prepared to have conversations with children on difficult topics. During the senior internship, teacher candidates complete community engagement activities (McDonald, 2007; McDonald et al., 2011) in each of the Bronfenbrenner (1981) Ecological Systems (Micro, Meso, Exo, and Macro). Microsystem tasks include talking with students who are the quietest, whom they know and like the least, and asking individual students what worries them; macrosystem tasks include grocery shopping, walking, and dining in their assigned school's neighborhood, reflecting on the opportunities they had as children compared with those their students have, and reflecting on the demographic composition of the school and community.

As a result of the design process, dual certification focus, and the specialty option, the EC/ECSE program became a model for the state of Maryland (Grasmick, 2015). Moreover, the state's master plan for teachers and providers of early childhood education (Maryland State Department of Education, 2015) now includes a recommendation that teacher education programs throughout the state develop dual certification programs with two focus areas: birth to age 5 and preschool to third grade.

The EC/ECSE program nonetheless only begins to touch upon the knowledge and skills that teachers need to respond to the social, emotional, and academic challenges in the classroom context due to lack of adult support, decreased resilience, and changes in brain structure associated with childhood trauma (Carrion et al., 2007; Dykman et al., 1997; Evans et al., 2008; Kim & Cicchetti, 2010; Shields & Cicchetti, 2001). While all teacher education programs can and should always improve and evolve, the demands of state and national accreditation and specialty program standards make a concerted focus on trauma- sensitive pedagogy a difficult, if not impossible, task. Therefore, teacher education programs should serve as a critical starting, but not final, point for developing trauma-sensitive pedagogy.

### 6.8.2  Trauma-Sensitive Pedagogy: An In-Service Example

There are numerous examples, varying in scope and focus, of trauma-sensitive professional development offerings for in-service educators, including Washington's SEL modules and the Massachusetts Advocates for Children's Safe and Supportive Schools Initiative. As previously stated, Washington's model is grounded in the professional development of individual teachers, while the Safe and Supportive Schools Initiative includes everyone in the entire school. Few would argue the merits of a whole-school focus, but resources often make this approach challenging, if not impossible in some settings.

Furthermore, evidence-based, trauma-sensitive teacher professional development curricula are scarce. Based on the prevalence of early childhood trauma, developmental consequences, and subsequent impacts on learning, the need to develop such curricula is of high importance. In response to this need, colleagues (one of whom authored this manuscript) from the University of Maryland and The

Pennsylvania State University (Panlilio & Tirrell-Corbin, 2017) developed a curriculum entitled Trauma-Sensitive Pedagogy (TSP), which is focused on those who work with young children from birth to age 8.

The TSP curriculum is grounded by the bioecological theory, which incorporates complicated and dynamic systems with educators as important members of the child's microsystem (Bronfenbrenner & Morris, 2006). This theory proposed that four interrelated and dynamic properties are involved in promoting growth and development: proximal processes, person, context, and time. Central to TSP are the dynamic processes between person-level and context-level (i.e., student and teacher) factors that, over time, influence specific developmental outcomes such as self-regulation that are important for academic success. Indeed, these proximal processes—student-teacher interactions or relatedness—have been implicated as the primary mechanism in promoting change and development. These processes are often most influential early in a child's life because it is through these interactions that children organize their set of cognitive, emotional, physiological, and behavioral responses to their world (Thelen & Smith, 2006). However, the influence of high-quality interactions between the child and his or her context remains important at later ages. For non-traumatized students, teacher-student relationships in kindergarten have been shown to influence work habits and grades by elementary school (Hamre & Pianta, 2001). For children in early elementary grades, their sense of relatedness with teachers predicts motivation and engagement in the classroom across school years (Furrer & Skinner, 2003).

Critical to the successful conceptualization and writing of professional development curricula for teachers (both pre- and in-service) is consideration of teachers' needs. Therefore, the content of TSP was grounded in the needs assessment responses of early childhood teachers (birth through third grade), early intervention specialists, early childhood specialists, and childcare center directors. Utilizing social media and personal email communications, the needs assessment was disseminated over a 3-month period. Respondents were asked to complete a needs assessment survey with a twofold purpose: to determine if stakeholders believed there to be sufficient need for TSP and to ascertain their recommendations for both the content and the structure of the curriculum. As previously stated, the support for TPS was overwhelmingly positive, with 98% agreeing or strongly agreeing that there is a need for trauma-sensitive professional development (Tirrell-Corbin et al., 2018).

TSP has been developed as a testable, trauma-sensitive curriculum designed as a classroom-level intervention, which provides educators with knowledge and skills to address the learning needs of young children who have experienced traumatic events. TSP learning experiences were designed around principles of adult learning theory (Cox, 2015; Knowles, 1973) and improvement science (Bryk et al., 2015). Lastly, in response to the data that suggest teachers experience secondary trauma as the result of working with children who have been traumatized (Alisic, 2012; Bride et al., 2004; Jennings & Greenberg, 2009; VanBergeijk & Sarmiento, 2006), TSP has been designed with a strong focus on reflections and self-care.

The curriculum has been designed to be delivered as a hybrid cohort model that combines in-person professional development sessions with online, interactive learning modules, and the formation of a virtual professional learning community within and across participating schools, school systems, and states. The online modules include substantive content regarding the impact of trauma on learning and behavior delivered via slide presentations, video presentations, virtual coaching, relevant resources such as websites and readings, and numerous opportunities for individual and cohort reflection. Learning through the online component will be assessed via project-developed measures. Program completers receive a certificate and, where applicable, continuing education credits/units. The six principles of improvement science (Bryk et al., 2015) serve as the TSP delivery framework. As a result, participants will explore a problem-of-practice through the systems of the bioecological theory using the Plan-Do-Study-Act cycle intrinsic to improvement science and aligned with principles of adult learning theory.

Given the startling statistics on the prevalence of childhood trauma (U.S. Department of Health and Human Services, 2017) combined with the academic (Rouse & Fantuzzo, 2009) and behavioral (Gilliam et al., 2016) consequences, it is imperative that schools and school systems heighten their support for teachers around trauma-sensitive pedagogy. While TSP serves as an example of an approach to informing and supporting educators who work with children who have experienced trauma, there is still much to be done at the microsystem level in order to ensure a positive trajectory for children who are otherwise at risk when it comes to their development and learning.

## 6.9   Conclusion

The African proverb "it takes a village to raise a child" serves as a powerful reminder of the many people and supports—the entire ecological system—necessary for a child to reach his, her, or their optimum potential. Therefore, we must include teachers and schools in our efforts to build a community of caring and supportive adults for children who are particularly vulnerable due to traumatic experiences. Teachers in particular are an important part of this "village," given the academic and the social influence that they have on children's development. In order to succeed, it is clear that teachers must be provided with the necessary tools and resources to be as effective as possible in promoting positive development for children with a history of trauma. While school-based microsystem efforts are powerful and essential, a full system of support for children who are vulnerable due to traumatic experiences must also be developed and supported, as is the case in Massachusetts (Massachusetts Safe and Supportive Schools Commission, 2017), at the macrosystem level.

# References

Alisic, E. (2012). Teachers' perspectives on providing support to children after trauma: A qualitative study. *School Psychology Quarterly, 27*, 51–59.

Atwoli, L., Stein, D. J., Koenen, K. C., & McLaughlin, K. A. (2015). Epidemiology of posttraumatic stress disorder: Prevalence, correlates and consequences. *Current Opinion in Psychiatry, 28*, 307.

Bride, B. E., Robinson, M. M., Yegidis, B., & Figley, C. R. (2004). Development and validation of the secondary traumatic stress scale. *Research on Social Work Practice, 14*, 27–35.

Bronfenbrenner, U. (1981). *The ecology of human development: Experiments by nature and design.* Boston, MA: Harvard University Press.

Bronfenbrenner, U., & Morris, P. A. (2006). The bio-ecological model of human development. In W. Damon & R. M. Lerner (Eds.), *Handbook of child psychology, Vol. 1: Theoretical models of human development* (6th ed., pp. 793–828). New York, NY: Wiley.

Brubacher, S. P., Powell, M. B., Snow, P. C., Skouteris, H., & Manger, B. (2016). Guidelines for teachers to elicit detailed and accurate narrative accounts from children. *Children and Youth Services Review, 63*, 83–92.

Bryk, A. S., Gomez, L. M., Grunow, A., & LeMahieu, P. G. (2015). *Learning to improve: How America's schools can get better at getting better.* Boston, MA: Harvard Education Press.

Carrion, V. G., Weems, C. F., & Reiss, A. L. (2007). Stress predicts brain changes in children: A pilot longitudinal study on youth stress, posttraumatic stress disorder, and the hippocampus. *Pediatrics, 119*, 509–516.

Cole, S. (2014). Implementing legal strategies for creating safe and supportive school environments. *Journal of Applied Research on Children: Informing Policy for Children at Risk, 5*, 1–22.

Cole, S. F., Eisner, A., Gregory, M., & Ristuccia, J. (2013). Helping traumatized children learn, *Vol. 2: Creating and advocating for trauma-sensitive schools.* Trauma and Learning Policy Initiative. Retrieved from http://www.traumainformedcareproject.org/resources/htcl-vol-2-creating-and-advocating-for-tss.pdf

Council for Exceptional Children. (2012). *CEC initial level special educator preparation standards.* Retrieved from https://www.cec.sped.org/~/media/Files/Standards/Professional%20Preparation%20Standards/Initial%20Preparation%20Standards%20with%20Elaborations.pdf

Council for the Accreditation of Educator Preparation. (2013). 2013 *CAEP standards.* Retrieved from http://caepnet.org/~/media/Files/caep/standards/caep-standards-one-pager-061716.pdf?la=en

Cox, E. (2015). Coaching and adult learning: Theory and practice. *New Directions for Adult and Continuing Education, 2015*(148), 27–38.

Division for Early Childhood. (2016). *Child maltreatment: A position statement of the Division for Early Childhood (DEC).* Washington, DC: DEC.

Dykman, R. A., McPherson, B., Ackerman, P. T., Newton, J. E. O., Mooney, D. M., Wherry, J., & Chaffin, M. (1997). Internalizing and externalizing characteristics of sexually and/or physically abused children. *Integrative Physiology and Behavioral Science, 32*, 62–74.

Evans, S. E., Davies, C., & DiLillo, D. (2008). Exposure to domestic violence: A meta-analysis of child and adolescent outcomes. *Aggression and Violent Behavior, 13*, 131–140.

Farrell, A., & Walsh, K. (2010). Working together for Toby: Early childhood student teachers engaging in collaborative problem-based learning around child abuse and neglect. *Australian Journal of Early Childhood, 35*, 53–62.

Flaherty, E. G., Sege, R., Price, L. L., Christoffel, K. K., Norton, D. P., & O'Connor, K. G. (2006). Pediatrician characteristics associated with child abuse identification and reporting: Results from a national survey of pediatricians. *Child Maltreatment, 11*, 361–369.

Florida State University Center for Prevention & Early Intervention Policy. (2014). *Trauma and toxic stress: Changing the trajectory for Florida's most vulnerable children to help them thrive* [Google Slides presentation]. Retrieved from http://floridatrauma.org/index.php

Furrer, C., & Skinner, E. (2003). Sense of relatedness as a factor in children's academic engagement and performance. *Journal of Educational Psychology, 95*, 148–162.

Gagnon, D. J., & Mattingly, M. J. (2012). *Beginning teachers are more common in rural, high-poverty, and racially diverse schools.* Retrieved from Carsey Institute website: https://scholars.unh.edu/cgi/viewcontent.cgi?article=1172&context=carsey

Gilliam, W. S., Maupin, A. N., Reyes, C. R., Accavitti, M., & Shic, F. (2016). Do early educators' implicit biases regarding sex and race relate to behavior expectations and recommendations of preschool expulsions and suspensions? *Yale Child Study Center, September*, pp. 991–1013.

Goldman, J. D. G., & Grimbeek, P. (2014). Reporting intervention preservice content preferred by student teachers. *Journal of Child Sexual Abuse, 23*, 1–16.

Grasmick, N. (2015, December 15). Md.'s perfect early childhood equation. *The Baltimore Sun.* Retrieved from http://www.baltimoresun.com/news/opinion/oped/bs-ed-grasmick-1220-20151219-story.html

Hamre, B. K., & Pianta, R. C. (2001). Early teacher-child relationships and the trajectory of children's school outcomes through eighth grade. *Child Development, 72*, 625–638.

Ingersoll, R., & Merrill, L. (2010). Who's teaching our children? *Educational Leadership, 67*(8), 14–20.

Jennings, P. A., & Greenberg, M. T. (2009). The prosocial classroom: Teacher social and emotional competence in relation to student and classroom outcomes. *Review of Educational Research, 79*, 491–525. https://doi.org/10.3102/0034654308325693

Jones Harden, B. (2015). *Services for families of infants and toddlers experiencing trauma: A research-to-practice brief* (OPRE Report No. 2015–14). Washington, DC: U.S. Department of Health and Human Services, Administration for Children and Families.

Kenny, M. C. (2004). Teachers' attitudes toward and knowledge of child maltreatment. *Child Abuse & Neglect, 28*, 1311–1319.

Kim, J., & Cicchetti, D. (2010). Longitudinal pathways linking child maltreatment, emotion regulation, peer relations, and psychopathology. *Journal of Child Psychology and Psychiatry, 51*(6), 706–716.

Klein, E. L., Tirrell-Corbin, C., & Lieber, J. (in press). Implementing a culturally responsive early childhood general/special education teacher preparation program through collaboration and continuous improvement. In I. Jones & M. Lin (Eds.), *Critical issues in early childhood teacher education, Vol. 1.* Charlotte, NC: IAP Press.

Knowles, M. (1973). *The adult learner: A neglected species.* Houston, TX: Gulf Publishing.

Kozol, J. (2012). *Fire in the ashes: Twenty-five years among the poorest children in America.* New York, NY: Broadway Books.

Lynch, M., & Cicchetti, D. (1992). Maltreated children's reports of relatedness to their teachers. *New Directions for Child and Adolescent Development*, 57, 81–107.

Maryland State Department of Education, Division of Early Childhood Development. (2015). *Report on developing a master plan on professional development for teachers and providers of early childhood education.* Retrieved from https://earlychildhood.marylandpublicschools.org/system/files/filedepot/21/pd_master_plan_report_-_final_jan_21_2016.pdf

Maryland State Department of Education, Division of Special Education and Early Intervention Services. (2016). *Strategic plan: Moving Maryland forward.* Retrieved from http://www.marylandpublicschools.org/programs/Documents/Special-Ed/DSEEISStrategicPlan2016.pdf

Massachusetts Safe and Supportive Schools Commission. (2017). *Fourth annual report.* Malden, MA: Massachusetts Department of Elementary and Secondary Education.

McDonald, M. (2007). The joint enterprise of social justice in teacher education: Dimensions of prospective teachers' opportunities to learn. *Journal of Teacher Education, 56*, 418–435.

McDonald, M. A., Tyson, K., Brayko, K., Bowman, M., Delport, J., & Shimomura, F. (2011). Innovation and impact in teacher education: Community-based organizations as field placements for preservice teachers. *Teachers College Record, 113*, 1668–1700.

Morgan, E., Salomon, N., Plotkin, M., & Cohen, R. (2014). *The school discipline consensus report: Strategies from the field to keep students engaged in school and out of the juvenile justice system*. New York, NY: Council of State Governments Justice Center.

National Association for the Education of Young Children. (2010). *2010 NAEYC standards for initial & advanced early childhood professional preparation programs*. Retrieved from https://www.naeyc.org/sites/default/files/globally-shared/downloads/PDFs/our-work/higher-ed/NAEYC-Professional-Preparation-Standards.pdf

National Child Traumatic Stress Network. (2003). *What is child traumatic stress?* Retrieved from https://www.nctsn.org/sites/default/files/resources//what_is_child_traumatic_stress.pdf

National Scientific Council on the Developing Child. (2005/2014). *Excessive stress disrupts the architecture of the developing brain: Working paper 3* (updated edition). Retrieved from www.developingchild.harvard.edu

Panlilio, C., & Tirrell-Corbin, C. (2017). Trauma sensitive pedagogy. In R. Svaricek (Ed.), *ICET 61st World Assembly: Re-thinking teacher professional education: Using research findings for better learning*. Czech Republic: Brno.

Rouse, H. L., & Fantuzzo, J. W. (2009). Multiple risks and educational well-being: A population-based investigation of threats to early school success. *Early Childhood Research Quarterly, 24*, 1–14.

Shields, A., & Cicchetti, D. (2001). Parental maltreatment and emotion dysregulation as risk factors for bullying and victimization in middle childhood. *Journal of Clinical Child Psychology, 30*, 349–363.

State of Washington Office of Superintendent of Public Instruction. (2018, March 28). *Social and emotional learning (SEL)*. Retrieved from http://www.k12.wa.us/StudentSupport/SEL/default.aspx

State of Washington Office of Superintendent of Public Instruction. (2018, May 25). *SEL online education module*. Retrieved from http://www.k12.wa.us/StudentSupport/SEL/OnlineModule.aspx

Thelen, E., & Smith, L. B. (2006). Dynamic systems theories. In W. Damon & R. M. Lerner (Eds.), *Handbook of child psychology, Vol. 1: Theoretical models of human development* (6th ed., pp. 258–312). New York, NY: Wiley.

Tirrell-Corbin, C., Panlilio, C., & Ferrara, A. (2018, July). *Responding to early childhood adversity: The necessity of trauma sensitive pedagogy in support of children, families and teachers*. Presentation at the 62nd World Assembly of the International Council on Education for Teaching, Laredo, TX.

U.S. Department of Health and Human Services, Administration for Children and Families, Administration on Children, Youth and Families, Children's Bureau. (2016). *Child maltreatment 2014*. Retrieved from https://www.acf.hhs.gov/sites/default/files/cb/cm2014.pdf

U.S. Department of Health and Human Services, Administration for Children and Families, Administration on Children, Youth and Families, Children's Bureau. (2017). *Child maltreatment 2015*. Retrieved from http://www.acf.hhs.gov/cb/resource/child-maltreatment-2015

VanBergeijk, E. O., & Sarmiento, T. L. L. (2006). The consequences of reporting child maltreatment: Are school personnel at risk for secondary traumatic stress? *Brief Treatment and Crisis Intervention, 6*, 79–98. https://doi.org/10.1093/brief-treatment/mhj00

Viezel, K. D., & Davis, A. S. (2014). Child maltreatment and the school psychologist. *Psychology in the Schools, 52*, 1–8.

Walkley, M., & Cox, T. L. (2013). Building trauma-informed schools and communities. *Children & Schools, 35*, 123–126.

Walter, H. J., Gouze, K., & Lim, K. G. (2006). Teachers' beliefs about mental health needs in inner city elementary schools. *Journal of the American Academy of Child & Adolescent Psychiatry, 45*, 61–68.

Wolpow, R., Johnson, M. M., Hertel, R., & Kincaid, S. O. (2009). *The heart of learning and teaching: Compassion, resiliency, and academic success.* Retrieved from http://www.k12.wa.us/CompassionateSchools/Resources.aspx

# Chapter 7
# Conclusions and Panel Discussion

Carlomagno C. Panlilio

## 7.1 Summary of the Current Volume

The chapters contained in this volume represent proceedings from the conference titled "Trauma-Informed Schools: How Child Maltreatment Prevention, Detection, and Intervention can be integrated into the School Setting," which was held from October 10 through 11, 2016. Each of the preceding chapter topics should be considered within the core elements of a trauma-informed school system framework (National Child Traumatic Stress Network, Schools Committee, 2017) and as a starting point in discussing how to begin the process of incorporating trauma-informed ideals into schools. In Chap. 1, Mary Pulido introduced the New York Society for the Prevention of Cruelty to Children (NYSPCC) and its role in providing treatment and support to families and children who have trauma histories of childhood abuse, neglect, and sexual abuse. She discussed NYSPCC's role in evaluating the Safe Touches program, a school-based sexual abuse prevention workshop for culturally and socioeconomically diverse students across kindergarten and the third grade. The Safe Touches Child Sexual Abuse Prevention Program curriculum and the study outcomes were discussed. A case study of the NYSPCC partnership with the Horace Mann School, in which comprehensive child sexual abuse prevention services for students, parents, and teachers were implemented, was also presented. Finally, the author discussed the process of replicating the Safe Touches program with the nonprofit ELIZA in Greece along with the preliminary results of the research team's pilot program.

In Chap. 2, Claire Crooks and David Wolfe introduced the Fourth R program aimed at teaching healthy relationships and decreasing risky behaviors in students between seventh and 12th grades. The Fourth R curriculum is designed to protect

C. C. Panlilio (✉)
Department of Educational Psychology, Counseling, and Special Education,
The Pennsylvania State University, University Park, PA, USA
e-mail: panlilio@psu.edu

© Springer Nature Switzerland AG 2019                                    109
C. C. Panlilio (ed.), *Trauma-Informed Schools*, Child Maltreatment Solutions
Network, https://doi.org/10.1007/978-3-030-12811-1_7

youth from the dangers related to sex, drugs, and violence. Importantly, the curriculum provides educators with the tools they need to address the concerns that parents may have about bullying, homophobia, drugs, alcohol, promiscuity, and mental illness. The authors discussed the results of several studies evaluating the program and its implementation process. Specifically, the authors reported that the Fourth R reduced dating violence, increased condom use, produced a buffering impact against violent delinquency among maltreated youth, and improved participants' communication skills and peer resistance abilities. Additional information on best practices and implementation was also discussed.

In Chap. 3, Brenda Jones Harden, Laura Jimenez Parra, and Aimee Drouin Duncan provided a framework for considering trauma's effects on children by providing a summary of the research on trauma exposure and outcomes for children across developmental and functional domains. Specifically, the authors covered the developmental sequelae across neurobiological, physical, motor, cognitive-academic, language, social-emotional, and mental health domains. Finally, the authors discussed the implications of early trauma exposure on school-based interventions. They provided an in-depth recommendation on how to translate knowledge of the developmental sequelae of trauma across Tiers 1–3 and how schools can respond accordingly through a trauma-informed framework.

In Chap. 4, Carlomagno Panlilio, Amanda Ferrara, and Leigha MacNeill explored the relationship between early adversity, self-regulation, and learning from the perspectives of developmental science and educational psychology. They argued for incorporating more proximal and dynamic views of learning as a framework for understanding mechanisms that lead to educational challenges experienced by maltreated children. Specifically, the authors identified self-regulation and self-regulated learning as two interrelated constructs that can help elucidate processes that result in maltreated students' academic vulnerability. The authors concluded the chapter with some suggestions regarding the incorporation of their conceptual framework with trauma-informed schools.

In Chap. 5, Susan Stone discussed the need to frame an understanding of maltreatment as a "wicked problem" defined by complex and unclear solutions. The level of complexity within wicked problems should take into account the potentially divergent aims across different systems such as child welfare, juvenile justice, education, and mental health, as well as the barriers posed by structural conditions such as poverty and racism. Understanding the social problem of maltreatment as complex necessitates the recognition that solutions may not be clear and straightforward. Therefore, there is a need for different child-serving systems to engage in a coordinated and collaborative manner when responding to maltreatment. This is particularly important when other child-serving systems must work collaboratively with the education system to address the academic needs of maltreated children. The author presented a perspective from which to consider the multiple contexts relevant to children who experience early maltreatment.

Finally, in Chap. 6, Christy Tirrell-Corbin provided an in-depth look at educational macro- and micro-level responses to childhood trauma. The author discussed current prevention models of mandated reporting practices in education and how these result in secondary stress for teachers. The author also provided recommendations for the creation of a trauma-sensitive pedagogy and examples of how this might be approached at the pre-service teacher preparation and in-service professional development levels.

## 7.2 Key Points

The final session of the conference consisted of an open discussion that engaged audience members in a dialogue with our panel members regarding the next steps toward promoting and implementing a trauma-informed framework in schools. Most, though not all, of those who presented their work at the conference produced a chapter for this volume (see Appendix A for the conference agenda). The remainder of this chapter is a summary of the panel discussion, which included all presenters at the conference. Out of respect for each panel member who presented, the names of those who responded to questions are not published in this section; rather, the discussions are summarized so as to protect the identities of those who asked questions and those who responded. These summaries were edited from the full transcript, and the interpretations provided are solely those of this chapter's author.

### 7.2.1 Cross-System Collaboration and Partnerships with Community and Family

The discussion session began with a dialogue about the importance of collaborative partnerships with multiple systems involved with children's education and the consideration of trauma-informed frameworks, highlighting core elements of the 2017 NCTSN System Framework for Trauma-Informed Schools. Specifically, partnerships with students and families, as well as cross-system collaboration and community partnerships. This includes being responsive to families in the local communities around their perception of trauma, engaging local schools in understanding their needs around responding to students' experiences of trauma, and how local communities and what resources are available.

Panel members underscored the importance of building partnerships with families. It is important to acknowledge that children are not experiencing traumatic events in a vacuum. On the contrary, there is evidence that intergenerational patterns of traumatic experiences are present across families (McDonnell & Valentino, 2016; Schwerdtfeger & Nelson Goff, 2007; Yehuda, Halligan, & Grossman, 2001). Therefore, any efforts to incorporate trauma-informed systems framework in schools must include parents, specifically parental supports. One example provided by panel members was the application of trauma-focused cognitive behavioral therapy (TF-CBT) in community settings (Cohen & Mannarino, 2008). Panel members discussed their experiences with TF-CBT implementation in specific communities that included parental participation during the child's therapy sessions. It was during these sessions that parents often recounted their own challenges as related to trauma. Given parents' own expressed limitations during these sessions, they have a harder time supporting their own children's behavioral changes at home and in school. It is therefore important to include parents and other caregivers who interact with the students in a whole system designed to incorporate the prevention and intervention efforts that address the sequelae of trauma.

Working within a systems framework for implementing trauma-informed approaches requires the promotion, if not the outright creation, of a cultural shift across all relevant systems. Panel members explained that a central goal of implementing trauma-informed systems in schools was to transform the schools' cultures. They argued that rather than viewing their framework as an intervention or program, creating trauma-sensitive schools through the flexible framework is, instead, a process that requires a cultural shift in how schools view and respond to student trauma (Cole, Eisner, Gregory, & Ristuccia, 2013). Another model that was offered during the discussion on cultural shift is one proposed by Comer (1980). The Comer School Development Program within Yale University's Child Study Center was developed and based on community involvement: the whole child was considered as a part of the broader school culture (Squires & Kranyik, 1995). In other words, a cultural shift is needed in order to view the relational aspects within schools and across stakeholders as important social capital in which society must invest (Comer, 2015).

The final point in discussing cross-system collaboration is that the power of communication within and across systems cannot be underestimated. Students who experienced early adversity oftentimes fall behind their non-traumatized peers in terms of academic performance due to poor coordination between systems. For example, poor communication between child welfare and school systems might lead to difficulties with transferring school records, continuing education accommodations, and course credits when foster children transfer placements (Day, Somers, Darden, & Yoon, 2015). Beyond schools, it is important for cross- system communication to occur in order to coordinate services that children and families may need to succeed in schools and communities. Therefore, collaborations that result in cross-system coalitions can provide much-needed support in the implementation of trauma-informed schools within a systems framework.

### 7.2.2   Concerns Around the Potentially Stigmatizing Nature of Traumatic Experiences

The next area of concern brought up to the panel by audience members centered on concerns around acknowledging trauma and potential stigmatizing effects of such efforts. Points of discussion in this section address the trauma-informed system core elements of identification and assessment, prevention and intervention related to traumatic stress, partnerships with students and families, creation of a trauma-informed learning environment, cultural responsiveness, crisis response, and cross-system collaboration and community partnerships. Panel members began by discussing the relationship between childhood trauma and mental health (Streeck-Fisher & van der Kolk, 2000), particularly the extent to which parents may object to their children's diagnoses due to the stigmatizing effects of mental health problems. Concerns especially focused on the potential challenge of providing access to mental health services in schools and communities when parents are wary of their children being stigmatized (Butler, 2014; Pescosolido et al., 2008).

Panel members reiterated the importance of Tier 1 universal prevention efforts that offer knowledge, tools, and procedures that can potentially mitigate stigma to everyone in the schools (e.g., Kellam et al., 2008). Other efforts to decrease stigma include protesting, education, public exposure, fostering group identity, and embracing "mental health" terms as positive concepts in public communications (Corrigan & Wassel, 2008; O'Connell, Boat, & Warner, 2009). One example of an effort to reduce stigma is the Positive Attitudes Toward Learning in Schools (PALS), which envisions families as partners with schools in order to improve children's academic, behavioral, and social functioning (Atkins, Graczyk, Frazier, & Abdul-Adil, 2003). By acknowledging and addressing possible stigma, those in need will be supported in accessing these services, particularly across each tier level of need.

A school within the San Diego Unified School District was discussed as an example of how a trauma-informed system of care could be implemented to successfully remove stigmatizing labels within the school. It was noted specifically that Godwin Higa, Principal of Cherokee Point Elementary School, implemented a trauma-informed approach within the school environment. He successfully created a Trauma Center within the school; working with parents in a culturally sensitive framework, involved them in the creation of a trauma-sensitive school; and shared his own experience of early childhood trauma to highlight hope for change (a video of the school can be found here: (https://traumasensitiveschools.org/cherokee-point-creates-a-trauma-sensitive-school-for-all-students). What is clear in the video is that the whole school community, even parents and children, openly discussed the issues related to trauma while taking stigma out of the picture.

## 7.2.3  Teacher Support

Given all of the ideas regarding the implementation of a trauma-informed system of support for students, families, and communities, it is also necessary to examine what the impacts are on teachers. The 2017 NCTSN System Framework recommends that teachers engage in additional training and efforts to become better prepared for trauma-informed teaching practices. The reality is that for many teachers, particularly those who work in areas that have a high prevalence of trauma, they are already burned out, stressed, and overworked, which often lead to experiencing secondary traumatic stress (Alisic, 2012). Secondary traumatic stress is an occupational hazard when providing direct services to traumatized populations, which includes features nearly identical to those of PTSD (Figley, 1999). Although the prevalence and consequences of secondary trauma in mental health and social service professionals have been examined, only a few studies have looked at this issue for teachers (e.g., Borntrager et al., 2012; Caringi et al., 2015). It is therefore important to integrate ways of assessing teacher outcomes into research studies or implementation programs, as well as to integrate teacher support into school-based interventions to mitigate any resulting burnout and secondary traumatic stress. This section addresses the need to consider the core element of teacher self-care and secondary traumatic stress within trauma-informed systems.

Panel members discussed a longitudinal study at Johns Hopkins University that involved evaluating the outcomes of the Good Behavior Game, an intervention that worked with teachers to develop classroom management skills and strategies for first-grade students in inner-city schools (Kellam et al., 2008, 2014). The authors found that due to the intervention, teachers were able to spend more time teaching rather than managing behavioral disruptions and therefore were able to enjoy their work more. These results highlight that it is not only important to understand the potential burden on teachers but also the potential benefits of engaging in trauma-informed prevention programs. When teachers are able to see evidence and concrete positive feedback, the quality of their own work can improve, which can potentially mitigate burnout and stress.

Additionally, high-quality professional development models can provide support for effective teaching practices (Kennedy, 2016) as well as overall mentoring support that can potentially mitigate the negative effects of secondary trauma. In Maryland, there is a mandate for a professional development school (PDS) model aimed at improving teacher practice and retention. An analysis of teacher retention rates was conducted comparing those who attended the PDS model versus those who did not. What panel members found was that after 5 years, schools that utilized the PDS model had a 90% retention rate versus less than 50% for those that did not utilize the model. Possible reasons for increased retention rates for teachers in schools that adopted the PDS model include the utilization of standards that provide uniform expectations across systems (e.g., Maryland PDS: http://mdk12.msde. maryland.gov/instruction/professional_development/standards/learning_forward. html) as well as a focus on shared responsibility for student achievement. These standards, in other words, promote faculty engagement in the daily activities of the entire school and not just what goes on within their classrooms. Additionally, this model includes a cohort of five teacher candidates in a school, along with their respective mentor teachers. Through the purposeful creation of this cohort of teacher candidates, support for each other and from their mentor teachers, and mentor teacher support from supervisors, the effects of burnout can be potentially avoided. Most, if not all of, student teacher placements are done in Title I schools, providing them with the experience of working in under-resourced communities and schools. Given the success of this PDS model, most student teachers are hired into their placement schools, and so these student teachers begin working in Title I schools with a support system already in place.

## 7.2.4  Assessments

Subsequent panel discussions focused on how schools and students would be assessed as a result of implementing a trauma-informed framework. For example, when looking at student performance outcomes, there was a sense that these performance measures are "moving targets" that change over the years. Are school districts expected to be measured by performance outcomes that yield graduation rates, proficiency in standardized test measures, or student growth per teacher in a tested subject? These metrics are important in measuring district performance, but the issue of how these outcome measures stack up in a trauma-informed framework remains a challenge. Although assessment concerns are not directly tied into the ten core elements of a trauma-informed framework, we propose that this issue is relevant for school policies.

One way to address the issue of a "moving target" recommended by panel members was to recommit to building trust with parents and inspiring and engaging students in school districts instead of worrying about more external metrics. The goal for each teacher, therefore, is to influence the interactions between student-teacher and parent-child to be more positive. The hope is that as a result of these more positive relationships, student performance will improve. Research does point to the importance of a teacher's socioemotional competence for positive interactions in the classroom (Jennings & Greenberg, 2009), which is then related to improved academic, behavioral, and emotional outcomes (Korpershoek, Harms, de Boer, van Kuijk, & Doolard, 2016).

Related to the earlier discussion about culture change being a goal of trauma-informed systems, a discussion ensued about shifting our conceptualization of assessments from quantitative performance measures to more process-oriented measures that incorporate an understanding of the degree to which a system changes its culture to be more in line with a trauma-informed or trauma-sensitive approach. For example, research on the effectiveness of the TLPI's Flexible Framework within trauma-sensitive schools was conducted through a partnership with a research firm that is examining the effectiveness of demonstration projects across schools in Massachusetts. Through this work, panel members observed that there is no framework in which to measure cultural transformation in schools. Despite the availability of quantitative and qualitative measures for general program evaluations, there appears to be a gap in how culture change is considered to be an important outcome of creating trauma-informed systems. To address this gap, one recommendation was to include the perspective of schools in how they would assess their own process of change through anecdotal and observational data. Panel members discussed the example of an assistant superintendent in a Massachusetts school district who, in an internal assessment of change, used observational data: she saw a teacher out on the

playground during recess playing with students who had never been observed playing before, the result of implementing a trauma-sensitive framework in that school.

## 7.2.5    Policy Linkages and School Discipline Policies

This section covers several core elements of trauma-informed systems that include
cultural responsiveness, school discipline policies and practices, and cross-system
collaboration and community partnerships. The panel discussed the issue of how to
begin advocating for trauma-informed schools at the policy level and recommended
being strategic in advancing a trauma-informed system framework. One example
provided was when the Education Committee Chair of a state approached one of the
panelists to address the issue of bullying. This became an opportunity to educate the
Education Committee Chair about the importance of whole school culture
approaches, which are as relevant to bullying as they are to the issue of trauma, and,
of course, these issues overlap (Kelleher et al., 2008). Subsequently, an anti-bullying
law that took a whole school approach into account was drafted by the committee
and subsequently passed. From that point forward, the Chair incorporated a whole
school approach in every bill proposed thereafter. In the state of another panel member, a similar process occurred when an anti-bullying law was being proposed.
Unfortunately, this proposed legislation sought to increase the school's punitive
responses to bullying behaviors. Advocacy for trauma-informed perspectives in this
legislative process required testimony on the impact that such laws would have on
children, particularly if the resulting disciplinary procedure would criminalize students from kindergarten through the twelfth grade. Similar to the previous example,
the Education Committee members of this state rolled back the proposal and considered the inclusion of relevant community and school stakeholders in creating a
trauma-informed response. The inclusion of community liaisons helps to account
for cultural sensitivity when it comes to trauma-informed responses.

With regard to school policy, an issue was raised regarding how to address truancy or the "invisible student" population within a trauma-informed framework.
Specifically, there was a question about what efforts are being made to reach out and
re-engage students prior to involvement with the juvenile justice system. This issue
is particularly salient given the evidence that early traumatic experiences are related
to increased truancy (Dembo et al., 2012). For children who experience abuse and
neglect, in particular, increased absenteeism has been related to disrupted placements either as a result of home removal or foster care placement (Leiter, 2007;
Zorc et al., 2013).

One recommendation was to form a truancy task force that includes multiple
stakeholders in the community such as local judges, doctors, and educators, among
others. For example, it is important to educate judges on possible reasons for student truancy, particularly as these relate to trauma. Another recommendation was to
examine truancy policies within schools, specifically the truancy letters that are sent
to students and families in order to assess the extent to which letters are punitive

versus inviting and collaborative. Third, it is important to look at truancy issues as problems related to student engagement. By conceptualizing truancy in relation to engagement, schools can implement programs that increase student participation and give them reasons to attend, whether that reason is related to academics, sports, music, art, or extracurricular activities.

A fourth recommendation to address truancy is to increase family engagement through home visits. In one example, elementary school teachers conducted home visits with their students' families. A majority of parents agreed to the visit and were surprised at the level of engagement that teachers showed. The visits provided teachers with insights into familial relationships and, more importantly, allowed teachers and family members to build a relationship. A final recommendation involved an activity where teachers wrote every student's name on a sticky note and placed these on a wall. During a faculty meeting, each teacher took a student's name off the wall with whom the teachers have a good relationship. Once completed, the entire faculty would then look at the names of the remaining students on the wall: the students without a connection in school. Once identified, teachers could then increase efforts to connect with these remaining students. Alternatively, teachers could also identify students that they know the least or the students with whom they do not connect and spend at least 15 minutes with these students in order to increase these students' connection with school.

## 7.2.6  Practical Strategies and Resources for Teachers

Given the amount of time and effort required to shift entire systems toward a more trauma-informed culture, it is important to provide teachers with practical strategies and resources, particularly strategies that teach empathy, *en route* to this cultural shift. The following recommendations were provided by panel members during the discussion:

*International Institute for Restorative Practices (IIRP)*
Faculty from the IIRP went into an urban Pennsylvania high school that was in chaos as evidenced by high truancy, poor classroom engagement, violence, and low achievement test scores. Within a year, the chaos had dropped by approximately 90%, and the academic achievement had risen because every adult in the school was taught how to deal with students in a particular empathic way. Every morning, children engaged in circles where everyone expressed their feelings to one another. By engaging in these practices, students learned that they had more in common than they did differences. Additionally, students learned how to resolve conflicts through a particular system of conflict resolution. Given these positive student outcomes, teachers could teach, the students were learning, and the violence disappeared. The following video describes the IIRP program in an Illinois middle school: www.iirp.edu/news-from-iirp/restorative-practices-in-an-illinois-middle-school.

*Crisis Prevention Institute (CPI) Training*
The training program offers skills on nonviolent crisis intervention in order to safely manage and prevent difficult or dangerous behaviors. According to panel members, their teachers who were trained in CPI methods increased their ability to recognize when a student is in crisis and exhibited increased sensitivity toward these students. By sending teachers to these trainings, it provided them with the necessary skills to respond to students in a trauma-informed manner. More information on the CPI program can be found on their website at hwww.crisisprevention.com/About-Us.

*Books and Other Resources*
An author named Susan Craig wrote several books that discuss classroom strategies that teachers could use when working with traumatized students. Below are examples of her work:

Craig, S. E. (2008). *Reaching and teaching children who hurt: Strategies for your classroom*. Baltimore, MD: Paul H. Brookes Publishing Co.
Craig, S. E. (2016). *Trauma-sensitive schools: Learning communities transforming children's lives, K-5*. New York, NY: Teachers College Press.

Sonia Nieto is another author that panelists recommended as a great resource for educators. Nieto's books encourage teachers to find the joy of learning and connect with what they love about their jobs that keep them going. Below are a few examples of her work:

Nieto, S. (2003). *What keeps teachers going?* New York, NY: Teachers College Press.
Nieto, S. (2005). *Why we teach*. New York, NY: Teachers College Press.
Nieto, S. (2014). *Why we teach now*. New York, NY: Teachers College Press.

In addition to these book recommendations, the National Center on Safe Supportive Learning Environments (NCSSLE) is another sound resource. The NCSSLE is funded by the Department of Education's (DoE) Office of Safe and Healthy Students and includes three main areas of support that include training, measurement and program implementation, and maintenance of the DoE School Climate Surveys. More information about the NCSSLE can be found at www.safe-supportivelearning.ed.gov/about.

Finally, the National Child Traumatic Stress Network (NCTSN) is an excellent resource for information about childhood trauma and the trauma-informed framework. The NCTSN was created by Congress in 2000 to raise the standard of care and increase access to services for children and families who are victims of traumatic events. The NCTSN is administered by the Substance Abuse and Mental Health Services Administration (SAMHSA) and is made up of a network of frontline providers, families, researchers, and national partners who are invested in improving the developmental trajectories of children who experience early traumatic stress. More information about the NCTSN can found at www.nctsn.org/.

## Conference Agenda for Trauma-Informed Schools

**Day 1: Monday, October 10, 2016**
*Nittany Lion Ballroom*

| | |
|---|---|
| 7:30–8:30 a.m. | Registration |
| | *Welcome* |
| 8:30–8:35 a.m. | Call to order |
| 8:35–8:55 a.m. | Introductory remarks and legislative changes<br>Network Director Jennie Noll, Ph.D., Penn State (8:35–8:45 am)<br>Provost Nicholas Jones, Ph.D., Penn State (8:45–8:55 am) |
| *Session I* | *Prevention*<br>Moderator: Jennie Noll, Ph.D., Penn State |
| 9:00 – 9:45 a.m. | *Elementary*: Mary Pulido, Ph.D., The New York Society for the Prevention of Cruelty to Children |
| 9:45–10:30 a.m. | *Middle school*: Elizabeth Letourneau, Ph.D., Director, Moore Center for the Prevention of Child Sexual Abuse/Johns Hopkins |
| 10:30–10:45 a.m. | *Break* |
| 10:45–11:30 a.m. | *High school*: David Wolfe, Ph.D., Director, CAMH Centre for Prevention Science/University of Toronto |
| 11:30–Noon | Open discussion |
| Noon–1:00 p.m. | *Lunch* |
| *Session II* | *Developmental impact of trauma*<br>Moderator: Erika Lunkenheimer, Ph.D., Penn State |
| 1:00–1:45 p.m. | Brenda Jones Harden, Ph.D., University of Maryland, College Park |
| 1:45–2:30 p.m. | Carlo Panlilio, Ph.D., Penn State |
| 2:30–2:45 p.m. | *Break* |
| 2:45–3:30 p.m. | Cristin Hall, Ph.D., Penn State |
| 3:30–4:00 p.m. | Open discussion |
| 4:00–4:05 | Day 1 Wrap-up: Jennie Noll, Ph.D., Penn State |

**Day 2: Tuesday, October 11, 2016**
*Nittany Lion Ballroom*

| | |
|---|---|
| 8:30 a.m. | Introductory Remarks<br>Network Director Jennie Noll, Ph.D., Penn State |
| *Session III* | *Improving educational efforts*<br>Moderator: Sheridan Miyamoto, Ph.D., Penn State |
| 8:35–9:15 a.m. | Brian Bliss, Ed.D., Superintendent, Solanco School District and Carlo Panlilio, Ph.D., Penn State |
| 9:15–10:00 a.m. | Susan Stone, Ph.D., University of California, Berkeley |
| 10:00–10:15 a.m. | *Break* |
| 10:15–11:00 a.m. | Bradley Stein, Ph.D., RAND Corporation/University of Pittsburgh |
| 11:00–11:30 a.m. | Open Discussion |
| 11:30–12:30 p.m. | *Lunch* |
| *Session IV* | *Breaking down barriers, identifying solutions and influencing policy*<br>Moderator: Carlo Panlilio, Ph.D., Penn State |
| 12:30–1:00 p.m. | Peter Simonsson, MSW, LCSW Director, Survivor Services/Joseph J. Peters Institute, Philadelphia |
| 1:00–1:30 p.m. | Joan Duvall-Flynn, Ed.D., PA NAACP |
| 1:30–2:00 p.m. | Christy Tirrell-Corbin, Ph.D., University of Maryland, College Park |
| 2:00–2:15 p.m. | *Break* |
| 2:15–2:45 p.m. | Michael Gregory, J.D., M.A.T., Clinical Professor of Law, Harvard Law School/Trauma and Learning Policy Initiative |
| 2:45–3:15 p.m. | Open discussion |
| *Panel* | *Panel discussion* |
| 3:15–4:15 p.m. | Speakers, plus session attendees, will convene in front of the conference audience to field questions, facilitate conversation, and enhance discussion |
| 4:15–4:20 p.m. | Closing Remarks: Jennie Noll, Ph.D. |

# References

Alisic, E. (2012). Teachers' perspectives on providing support to children after trauma: A qualitative study. *School Psychology Quarterly, 27,* 51–59.

Atkins, M. S., Graczyk, P. A., Frazier, S. L., & Abdul-Adil, J. (2003). Toward a new model for promoting urban children's mental health. *School Psychology Review, 32,* 503–514.

Borntrager, C., Caringi, J. C., van den Pol, R., Crosby, L., O'Connell, K., Trautman, A., & McDonald, M. (2012). Secondary traumatic stress in school personnel. *Advances in School Mental Health Promotion, 5,* 38–50. https://doi.org/10.1080/1754730X.2012.664862

Butler, A. M. (2014). Shared decision-making, stigma, and child mental health functioning among families referred for primary care-located mental health services. *Families, Systems, & Health, 32,* 116–121.

Caringi, J. C., Stanick, C., Trautman, A., Crosby, L., Devlin, M., & Adams, S. (2015). Secondary traumatic stress in public school teachers: Contributing and mitigating factors. *Advances in School Mental Health Promotion, 8,* 244–256. https://doi.org/10.1080/1754730X.2015.1080123

Cohen, J., & Mannarino, A. P. (2008). Disseminating and implementing Trauma-Focused CBT in community settings. *Trauma, Violence, & Abuse, 9,* 214–226.

Cole, S. F., Eisner, A., Gregory, M., & Ristuccia, J. (2013). Creating and advocating for trauma-sensitive schools. Retrieved from https://traumasensitiveschools.org/tlpi-publications/

Comer, J. (1980). *School power: Implications of an intervention project.* New York, NY: Free Press.

Comer, J. (2015). Developing social capital in schools. *Society, 52*, 225–231.

Corrigan, P. W., & Wassel, A. (2008). Understanding and influencing the stigma of mental illness. *Journal of Psychosocial Nursing and Mental Health Services, 46*, 42–48.

Day, A. G., Somers, C., Darden, J. S., & Yoon, J. (2015). Using cross-system communication to promote educational well-being of foster children: Recommendations for national research, practice, and policy agenda. *Children & Schools, 37*, 54–62.

Dembo, R., Briones-Robinson, R., Ungaro, R., Gulledge, L., Karas, L., Winters, K. C., … Greenbaum, P. E. (2012). Emotional/psychological and related problems among truant youths: An exploratory latent class analysis. *Journal of Emotional and Behavioral Disorders, 20*, 157–168.

Figley, C. R. (1999). Compassion fatigue: Toward a new understanding of the costs of caring. In B. H. Stamm (Ed.), *Secondary traumatic stress: Self-care issues for clinicians, researchers, and educators* (2nd ed., pp. 3–28). Lutherville, MD: Sidran.

Jennings, P. A., & Greenberg, M. T. (2009). The prosocial classroom: Teacher social and emotional competence in relation to student and classroom outcomes. *Review of Educational Research, 79*, 491–525. https://doi.org/10.3102/0034654308325693

Kellam, S. G., Brown, C. H., Poduska, J. M., Ialongo, N. S., Wang, W., Toyinbo, P., … Wilcox, H. C. (2008). Effects of a universal classroom behavior management program in first and second grades on young adult behavioral, psychiatric, and social outcomes. *Drug and Alcohol Dependence, 95*(Suppl 1), S5–S28.

Kellam, S. G., Wang, W., Mackenzie, A. C. L., Brown, C. H., Ompad, D. C., Or, F., … Windham, A. (2014). The impact of the Good Behavior Game, a universal classroom-based preventive intervention in first and second grades, on high-risk sexual behaviors and drug abuse and dependence disorders into young adulthood. *Prevention Science, 15*(Suppl 1), S6–S18.

Kelleher, I., Harley, M., Lynch, F., Arseneault, L., Fitzpatrick, C., & Cannon, M. (2008). Associations between childhood trauma, bullying and psychotic symptoms among a school-based adolescent sample. *British Journal of Psychiatry, 193*, 378–382. https://doi.org/10.1192/bjp.bp.108.049536

Kennedy, M. M. (2016). How does professional development improve teaching? *Review of Educational Research, 86*, 945–980. https://doi.org/10.3102/0034654315626800

Korpershoek, H., Harms, T., de Boer, H., van Kuijk, M., & Doolard, S. (2016). A meta-analysis of the effects of classroom management strategies and classroom management programs on students' academic, behavioral, emotional, and motivational outcomes. *Review of Educational Research, 86*, 643–680. https://doi.org/10.3102/0034654315626799

Leiter, J. (2007). School performance trajectories after the advent of reported maltreatment. *Children and Youth Services Review, 29*, 363–382.

McDonnell, C. G., & Valentino, K. (2016). Intergenerational effects of childhood trauma: Evaluating pathways among maternal ACEs, perinatal depressive symptoms, and infant outcomes. *Child Maltreatment, 21*, 317–326.

National Child Traumatic Stress Network, Schools Committee. (2017). *Creating, supporting, and sustaining trauma-informed schools: A system framework.* Los Angeles, CA/Durham, NC: National Center for Child Traumatic Stress.

O'Connell, M. E., Boat, T., & Warner, K. E. (Eds.). (2009). *Preventing mental, emotional, and behavioral disorders among young people: Progress and possibilities.* Washington, D.C.: National Academies Press.

Pescosolido, B. A., Jensen, P., Martin, J. K., Perry, B. L., Olafsdottir, S., & Fettes, D. (2008). Public knowledge and assessment of child mental health problems: Findings from the National Stigma Study-Children. *Journal of the American Academy of Child & Adolescent Psychiatry, 47*, 339–349.

Schwerdtfeger, K. L., & Nelson Goff, B. S. (2007). Intergenerational transmission of trauma: Exploring mother-infant prenatal attachment. *Journal of Traumatic Stress, 20*, 39–51.

Squires, D. A., & Kranyik, R. D. (1995). The Comer Program: Changing school culture. *Educational Leadership, 53*, 29–32.

Streeck-Fisher, A., & van der Kolk, B. (2000). Down will come baby, cradle and all: Diagnostic and therapeutic implications of chronic trauma on child development. *Australian & New Zealand Journal of Psychiatry, 34*, 903–918.

Yehuda, R., Halligan, S. L., & Grossman, R. (2001). Childhood trauma and risk for PTSD: Relationship to intergenerational effects of trauma, parental PTSD, and cortisol excretion. *Development and Psychopathology, 13*, 733–753.

Zorc, C. S., O'Reilly, A. R., Matone, M., Long, J., Watts, C. L., & Rubin, D. (2013). The relationship of placement experience to school absenteeism and changing schools in young, school-aged children in foster care. *Children & Youth Services Review, 35*, 826–833.

# Index

© Springer Nature Switzerland AG 2019
C. C. Panlilio (ed.), *Trauma-Informed Schools*, Child Maltreatment Solutions
Network, https://doi.org/10.1007/978-3-030-12811-1

Printed in the United States
By Bookmasters